IN STITCHES

IN STITCHES

Una Stubbs

WARD LOCK LIMITED · LONDON

With love to Jason, Christian, Joe and Nicky.

First published in Great Britain in 1984
by Ward Lock Limited, 82 Gower Street,
London WC1E 6EQ, a Pentos Company.

Designed by Bob Swan
Text set in Plantin Light/Semi Bold
by Advanced Filmsetters (Glasgow) Ltd

Printed and bound in Italy by
Sagdos, SpA Milan

British Library Cataloguing in Publication Data

Stubbs, Una
    Una Stubbs in stitches.
    1. Embroidery
    I. Title
    746.44   TT770

ISBN 0–7063–6303–5

Contents

A Stitch in Time

Most of us have vague memories of doing needlework at school – my own hazy recollection is of making pink poplin knickers – but, somehow or other, it usually gives way to other interests.

Those who feel faint stirrings again many years on are perhaps discouraged by the high standards some textbooks appear to demand. Others simply feel disheartened after wrestling for twenty-four hours with a felt waistcoat they would not be seen dead in anyway.

What they really yearn to do is to make the things *they* want to make, in a way that looks both pretty and professional. And this is not only possible but, with a little time and application, easier than you think.

I started embroidery twelve years ago when I was pregnant. Heavy with child wasn't the word for it, so I bought some linen, a needle and silks, and started from scratch.

It quite simply changed my life. I am not a temperamental person, but I find that the little roll-up embroidery kit I carry in my handbag helps me to cut off from pressure. I can always be found somewhere in a studio corner, deeply engrossed in drawn threadwork or a new design.

On location for Worzel Gummidge, Jon Pertwee teasingly used to call me Bessie Bland, and ask why I never got angry. It's a secret I happily pass on to anyone.

I have heard of men taking up needlework but, traditionally, it is a woman's craft. When you discover that the prime requirements are patience, logic and a cool head, you no longer wonder why!

It is also an art form, and a rewarding means of self-expression that has a way of easing tension and pushing life's hustle and bustle into perspective. It takes less time to make a little sketch and plan a piece of work than it does to queue up in a surgery for valium.

Once, when I was lazing on a holiday beach in Greece – soaking up the sun and, as usual, doing a little embroidery – an American woman struck up a conversation. It soon became clear that she had terrible problems. She seemed under great strain and on the verge of a breakdown.

We talked about needlework. Before long, she was back on the beach with some fabric and a needle and thread, trying her first tentative stitches. After that, whenever I saw her, she was totally absorbed in her embroidery.

At the end of the week, after she had checked out of the hotel, the manager handed me an envelope. Inside it I found a gold ring, and a note which said simply: 'You saved my life.'

Needlework, of course, demands time – a priceless commodity in all our lives. I have no housekeeper or secretary; I think I would feel guilty letting someone else do the cleaning whilst I sat and sewed, because I mostly love solitude.

At home I look after my three sons and do everything myself. Like anyone else, I have difficulty finding time but over the years I have evolved my own system of buying the precious hour or two I need.

In the mornings I go through the housework like a blur, and keep fit by running up and down stairs – spurred on by the prospect of a blissful, tranquil period to myself. You *can* make time if you want to.

I consider bringing up my family to be my most important job, but needlework helps to make home a haven for us; a place to retreat to at the end of a busy day, closing the front door on the world. I often embroider in the evenings while my sons watch telly, or paint or read.

I have become so immersed in needlework that there are many times when I take stitch books to bed and mull through them, planning my next piece. Far more relaxing than Gothic romances, I might add!

One of the occupational hazards of needlework is that onlookers have a habit of interrupting to ask what you are doing. Be prepared – people cannot resist a peep. So it is important not to be self-conscious about your work; don't worry that it isn't perfect.

If Auntie Florrie turns your embroidery over to study the back – slap her wrist and tell her it's none of her business.

You will be really quite surprised how your confidence grows. I have come to regard the curious critic not as off-putting but as a spur to a beautiful finished product.

Apart from having been shown how to thread a needle, I have never been taught needlework. Everything I know I learned as I went along.

It is, however, necessary to approach needlework in the right way. Forget other people's comments if you wish to avoid chronic anxiety.

I enjoy doing the work by hand because it is so relaxing. The first requirement of the art of needlework is positively to relish taking your time. Organize your day so that you anticipate an hour of complete self-indulgence. Planning with anticipation puts the unimportant things firmly where they belong.

You will find it helpful to surround yourself with attractive work-tools, such as little boxes and pin cushions. I have gathered tiny containers and tools that are both workmanlike and pleasing. They need not be expensive – the scissors I use for broderie anglaise are made from tin, a present from my son. Collecting beautiful silks and miniature beads is a joy in itself. The more attractive everything you use is, the more artistic your approach becomes.

The right approach also involves thinking a couple of generations ahead. Needlewomen of years gone by created work that is still serviceable today. With patience, and a little iron resolve, their unhurried skills can be resurrected. In some ways, we probably need them more than ever.

Once you have invested your time and developing talents in it, your work should still be around a century from now. But your efforts will only be repaid if you use pure, natural fabrics. Man-made materials may prove in the long term to be not only a disappointment, but also an expensive mistake.

There is nothing quite like finishing a piece I have worked on for weeks, perhaps in a dozen different places, and giving it a good, old-fashioned, Dolly Blue laundering. The pleasurable smell of steam and starch and the feel of well-pressed linen are quite baffling to the uninitiated.

Needlework is a gentle dedication. A creative, feminine art inspiring a sense of fulfilment. In some small way I hope I can persuade you to take it up – perhaps for the second time round – and go on to do better than me.

I pass on a few tips, not as an instructor, but more of a sister, aunt and granny all rolled into one. I'm not a technically perfect needlewoman – just a friend with an urge to push you into having a go, and give you the encouragement to carry on.

Tips and Tools

A piece of beautiful needlework can be embroidered with the minimum of tools, but I found that, as my interest grew, so did my collection of useful odds and ends. The small work-basket I started out with has spilled over into tins, boxes and a drawerful of scraps. Unlike some hobbies, needlework does not have to be bundled up and hidden away. Pretty work containers and embroidery frames enhance a room.

I work only with pure fabrics – linens, cottons and silks – which I buy from Liberty. It may cost a little more, but the store has a peaceful atmosphere, and being surrounded by lovely fabrics puts me in just the right frame of mind for needlework.

My work-boxes are crammed with an assortment of useful things. One basket contains embroidery silks in graded shades of colour. Another is overflowing with a jumble of loose strands. I have a jackdaw policy of never throwing anything away. A brief rummage often produces exactly the thread I was looking for.

Needles and threads

I keep lots of needles of all sizes in a little tin. You should always choose the best quality as they last longer, and try to keep embroidery needles (they have a larger eye) separate from plain sewing needles.

Coarse and heavy fabrics should generally be worked with a thicker needle and thread, while delicate fabrics need a finer needle and fewer strands of thread.

When you buy packets of good-quality assorted needles – they are easy to come across in needle-work shops and haberdashery departments – try to store the needles in their original wrappings, which are designed to protect needle points and keep them rust-free.

If you are ever unsure about which needle-size or thread-thickness to use, make a few trial stitches on a scrap of fabric. In the long term it may save time and trouble. Even beautifully-made stitch-work can be dulled by using too thick or thin a thread.

Whenever I work with stranded silks I generally use about three strands if the fabric is of medium weight and quality. This, of course, can be varied to create different effects.

For instance, to raise or pad a satin stitch I do not use a thicker thread, but lay a foundation of running or daisy stitch. Alternatively, a few extra strands can be used to give French knots a chunky texture, but I twist them only once round the needle instead of twice.

Coats publish small handbag-size books of stitches, which I always carry around for quick reference. Once the basic stitches become familiar, you can add variations of your own to achieve the effect you want.

Starting and finishing threads

Finishing on the underside of your fabric is no problem, but starting a thread often can be. Knots, especially on delicate materials, look lumpy when the work has been pressed.

A good tip I picked up is to insert the needle on the right side, a little away from my stitching, leaving a shortish thread. Work the area of embroidery and finish off with a few tiny darning stitches on the underside. Then you can draw the original thread to the underside, and darn in. Finishing stitches should be as flat as possible and not too close together. Any excess thread can be snipped away.

Above *If you keep all your embroidery silks, needles, and most frequently-used tools in a large basket, you will be spared the frustration of having to hunt high and low for equipment every time you pick up your work. Remember, embroidery is meant to be peaceful and relaxing.*

Opposite *It is a good idea to keep any scraps of fabric together, in a large drawer for instance. They can then be used at a later date for small embroidery projects, such as making a pin cushion.*

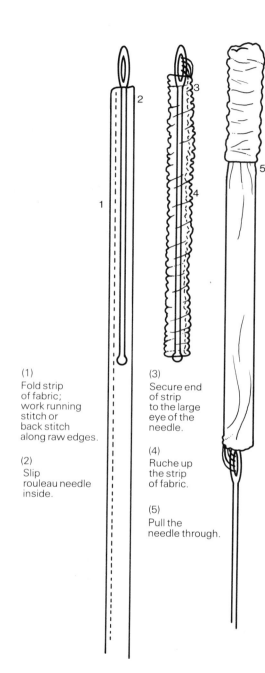

(1)
Fold strip
of fabric;
work running
stitch or
back stitch
along raw edges.

(2)
Slip
rouleau needle
inside.

(3)
Secure end
of strip
to the large
eye of the
needle.

(4)
Ruche up
the strip
of fabric.

(5)
Pull the
needle through.

Using your rouleau needle

Fabrics

Some natural fabrics are expensive, but if you use them your embroidery will last several lifetimes and become a family heirloom. Some of the projects outlined later are designed to be handed down – table-cloths signed by the family to commemorate weddings and birthdays, embroidered pictures recalling favourite holidays, and so on.

If you can't afford linen, or it is hard to find locally, buy some calico instead. There is quite a range available so you should be able to find something that suits the work you want to do.

You should really make clothes that do not date. In my work I have to wear lots and lots of them, and they are always on show. So when I make things for myself I choose classic styles which do not move in and out of fashion. I like constants that always look good and wear well. And this is the real beauty of natural fabric. Look how you can wear shirts, such as little crepe blouses from junk shops, years and years after they were made.

Fabric widths can vary enormously, depending on what they are intended for. The most commonly-used are found in 36, 45, 48, 54, and 60 in widths.

Always check carefully that the fabric has been pre-shrunk. If it hasn't been, wash it according to the instructions before cutting out. Hours of work can be completely ruined by shrinkage, for which the only answer, unfortunately, is to stand in the corner and silently weep.

If the fabric has no clearly-defined right or wrong side, mark the reverse with a pin or discreet pencil cross. Then, when each separate piece is made up, any slight difference will be unobtrusive.

Tools

One of my most useful pieces of equipment is a magnifying glass, which I use for fine work. It hangs round my neck leaving both hands free, and has two lenses, one of them very powerful. They can be bought for under £5 from most shops that cater in some way for stamp collectors. Absolutely invaluable.

For eyelet work I use a stiletto to push holes in the fabric. In some shops they are known as awls. They have a grippable wooden handle, but are dangerously sharp – I push mine into a cork when not in use.

I have a thing about needlework shops – I just can't walk past one without buying something, even if it is only a new packet of beads for 20p.

One of my favourite tools is a rouleau needle, about 6 in long with a knob at the end. Hats off to whoever invented them – they are unbeatable for turning narrow tubes of fabric, such as shoulder-straps, the right way out after seaming.

Apart from specialist shops and the Royal School of Needlework, they can be hard to track down. If you have no luck, try a knitter's needle, which has a blunt end and a wide eye.

Among my handy oddments I have a tiny screwdriver, ideal for tightening ring frames: and soft and hard pencils, a sharpener and a rubber, which I use for sketching and transferring designs.

A stitch-ripper with a bobble end is one of the few modern needlework inventions of genius. It is ideal for unpicking and correcting mistakes without tearing the fabric.

I also keep a few acrylic paints for touching up canvas or linen pictures, especially faces. Often a little blush pink in the right place looks more effective than heavily embroidered features.

A small assortment of scissors is necessary: large ones for cutting out, and a pointed pair for scalloping and doing buttonholes. The orange-handled ones are the best, but they are so hideous that I have to hide them in the drawer. I find I use my old tin pair most of all.

The prettiest and most practical tape-measure I've yet to find came from the Royal School of Needlework shop. It looks like a wooden spinning-top and has a tiny winder.

My son made a wooden pencil box at woodwork class when he was nine. I use it for beads, which I collect wherever I go. If they are very small I use a beading needle, which bends slightly. They are available in packets of assorted sizes.

I keep my fabric scraps trimmed and folded in a large drawer, so that when I come to dip into them they always look appetizing.

I made my own pin cushion from scraps, which is far more satisfying than buying one. Should you wish to try your hand at one, I have included a simple pattern (pages 40–42).

Ring frames are inexpensive and essential for keeping an even tension and eliminating puckering. Sizes vary, but I find the 4 in, 6 in, 8 in and 10 in most practical. Frames, especially the larger swivel types and table-top versions, are ideal for drawn threadwork and larger pieces of work (and quite impressive if Auntie Florrie drops in). In place of a large frame you can buy an old wooden picture frame from a junk shop and fasten your fabric to it with drawing pins. I'm told it works equally well.

When a frame is used the fabric is stretched fairly tightly within it, so it is difficult to pass the needle in and out of your work in one movement.

Although most stitch books have to be illustrated in that way, your thread should be pulled completely through on the right side and on the wrong side of the fabric during each stitch.

When I am travelling or working I take my roll-up kit everywhere with me. It was bought by my sister and thoughtfully includes space for needles, scissors, silks, beads and a travelling pencil. Together with one of the Coats pocket stitch books and my small sketch book, I have more than enough to make my work-breaks restful and rewarding.

I have a small silver thimble which I do not use very often, except perhaps when working on very tough fabric. (I embroidered Dennis the Menace on my son's denim jacket some years ago.) For anyone who needs a thimble, but can't seem to adapt to one, a pad of sticking plaster on your finger often helps.

I have a small library of needlework books in my kitchen, and I find them a pleasure and a constant source of inspiration. Old stitchwork books are particularly fascinating. I have made several lucky finds browsing in second-hand bookshops.

Most importantly, do invest in a good lamp to work by. Some embroidery is very fine, and tiring on the eyes. Make the most of sunshine too – summer holidays are ideal for needlework outdoors.

Samplers

Before the days of pocket stitch books, needle-women recorded their repertoire of stitches on samplers. They are still an invaluable aid for the budding embroidery designer; indeed anyone taking up needlework should consider starting one.

Each new stitch you learn can be practised in a row on the sampler. As the rows increase, it becomes a living source of reference, far better in fact than any text book.

You could even keep two samplers permanently on table-top frames – one for embroidery stitches, the other for drawn counted threadwork.

Leave them out in your work-room and when you design a piece of work you have a ready-made stitch guide. It is also useful to hang a small note-book with ribbon or silk on your sampler frame for a record of stitch styles, with your observations on each. Just think, you could even frame it and write underneath, 'This is my first sampler – rotten isn't it?'

Practical work is the best and easiest way of building a knowledge of needlework.

Museums all over Britain take a great interest

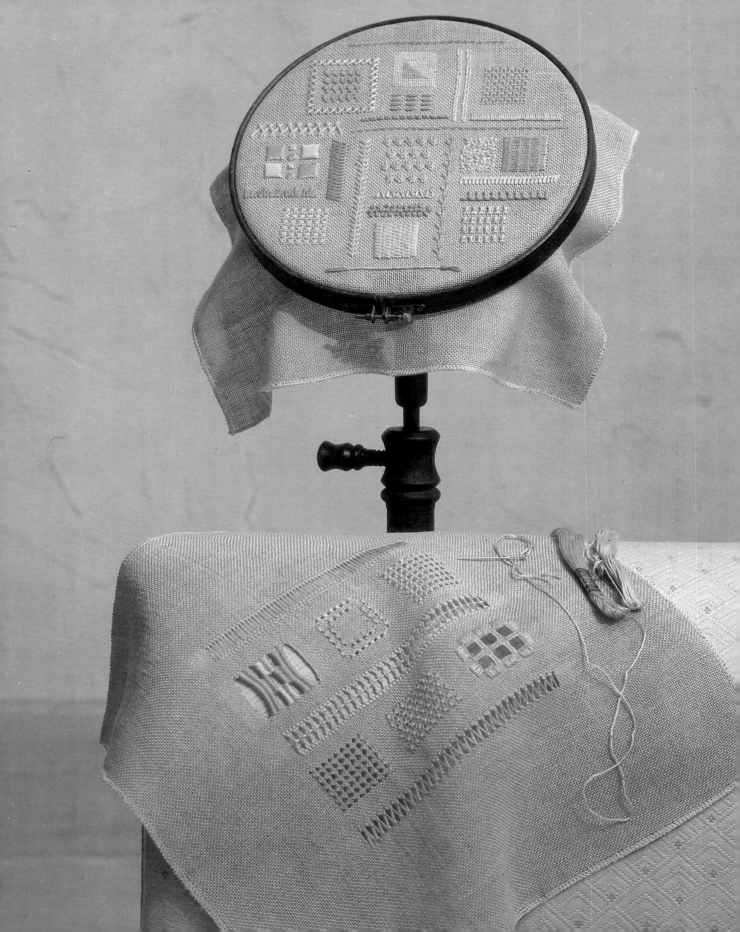

in costume and displays of historical and regional stitchcraft. It is a hobby of mine to carry a notebook for sketches and ideas I pick up on my travels.

Once you start embroidery, or any other art form, it makes you notice things you would normally pass by.

Design

Anything that sparks off a train of creative ideas is worth keeping. I have a folder that I fill with sketches – wild flowers, old pictures from Elle – anything in fact which sets me thinking. Over the years I have added pieces of antique embroidery from shops and jumble sales for inspiration.

When you have a design in mind, the most important rule is to think through your needle. Whatever you draw will eventually have to be translated into stitches. It takes practice, but the knack is to visualize the finished piece as you create it.

Traditional embroidery patterns tend to have a central motif surrounded by a rhythm of natural flowing lines. It is a pleasant style to familiarize yourself with, and can help you to produce some beautiful designs.

The creation of embroidery pictures is another technique that we shall look at more fully later. Whatever you try, the important thing is to have a go.

Transferring your design

There are methods, using graph paper, which I confess have always left me baffled. I work out a design in my sketchbook and then draw it lightly in pencil directly onto the fabric, outlining it more distinctly when I feel it is right.

The thought of this may at first give you the jitters but, fear not, there is an easy method using carbon paper. It is so simple that you can even use it to transfer your children's drawings for embroidering.

Pin your fabric down on a smooth surface and place your paper design over it in the right position. Then pin the paper to the fabric – but only down the right-hand side – so that it can be opened like a book cover.

Between the two, slip a sheet of carbon paper, face down. Do not pin the carbon to the fabric as it will leave a mark. Hold down firmly and trace over your design with a pencil – use a sharp point for fine fabrics and a thicker point for coarse material.

When you have finished, lift the carbon carefully to check that you have transferred the whole pattern. Once you have begun stitching, it is very frustrating to discover that you have missed a line.

To 'fix' the design to the fabric, and prevent smudging, remove the carbon and pattern paper, cover with clean tissue paper and press with a warm iron.

Scalloping

A shaped, embroidered edge gives an attractive finish to a range of things, from table-cloths to lingerie.

If you have a good needlework shop locally, you may be able to obtain scalloping transfers. I find it more satisfying to design my own to fit the outline I am working on.

Whichever method you choose, take care never to work to the very edge of the fabric as this makes it very difficult to sew, hard to cut away, and likely to end up looking lumpy.

Making your own scalloping is enjoyable and easy. On your pattern paper draw a straight line or curve, depending on what you are making, for the line you want your scallops to follow.

A small button or coin can be used as a template, and use a pencil so that you can rub out any clangers. For decorative corners use coins of different sizes, or a cardboard template.

Draw an inner line as well as an outer one for each curve – easily done by sliding the coin towards you slightly – to serve as a stitch guide.

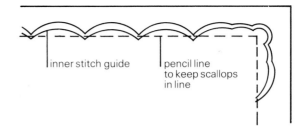

inner stitch guide   pencil line
to keep scallops
in line

Opposite *A sampler is a record of your repertoire of stitches and can be a great help when planning a new embroidery design. I like to keep two samplers; the one in the table-top frame is for embroidery stitches and the other is for drawn counted threadwork.*

Transfer your pattern using carbon paper and remember to allow some room on the fabric edges for cutting away after stitching. Cover the carbon outlines with clean tissue paper and press with a warm iron to 'fix' the design.

Work a *running stitch* inside the scallops to give the finished work some body, and then *buttonhole stitch* closely around the curves. The loops lie on the outer edge where the fabric is to be cut away.

Never cut a scallop before it is complete. If you really can't wait, do not cut the first scallop until you have completed the second and so on.

Buttonholes

Many needlewomen find buttonholes tedious to sew, but it is worth spending time perfecting them, if only because they have a knack of drawing the eye to the line of the garment. Neat buttonholes give a clean edge to your work and are really not at all the headache they sound.

If you follow one or two basic rules everything else falls into place. The obvious one, which I am sure you know (but nevertheless I often have to work it out), is that women's clothes button right over left and men's the opposite way.

Be careful when cutting the buttonhole slit – a fraction too long and it will slip open too easily. Use this simple method and avoid facing your public half undressed:

Place your first button at the top of the button-hole strip, centre it, and make a small pencil mark on either side. Remove the button, join the two marks and cut. Make the line just $\frac{1}{8}$ in wider than the button for a perfect fit.

 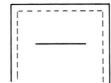

pencil mark

Start the buttonhole stitch at the end farthest from the fabric edge.

Work two small backstitches on the wrong side and draw the needle through the open buttonhole slit. Stitch from left to right and put a bar of stitches at each end for reinforcement. Practical steps are also explained in the granny cami project (page 105).

Pressing

When ironing your embroidery, take care not to flatten the raised stitchwork. Always press on the reverse side to preserve the texture. Lay your work face down on a thick, padded surface such as a blanket, which has been covered with a piece of cotton. This method is ideal for pressing lace too.

Linen should not be sprayed or dampened – cover with a damp cloth instead, again ironing on the wrong side of the work.

Always press on the reverse whenever possible, and remove any tacking first. If you have to press a piece on the right side during making up, test the iron heat on a scrap first, and cover the work with a cloth.

Drawn threadwork

One day I plan to devote a lot of time to drawn threadwork. It is so absorbing that I would really like to improve at it. Perfection, I'm afraid, will have to wait until I am not so busy and the children are at a different age.

Drawn threadwork is almost a neglected art today, but well worth keeping alive. It is lovely to do in the garden in the summertime because you do make a mess with all the threads.

I have included a selection of drawn thread embroidery in the glossary. To draw threads in preparation you need to mark pencil guidelines on the fabric. Always use a frame for the actual stitchwork.

Begin by lifting a thread in the middle of the guideline with your needle point. Ease it gently up and snip. If you are making a square border, draw each half of the thread out, a little at a time, towards each corner.

If you work with the thread facing you horizontally you will avoid confusing the warp and weft and drawing the wrong thread.

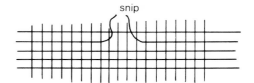

snip

When each half of the snipped thread has been withdrawn, it must be threaded onto a needle and darned outwards into the corners, finishing on the wrong side of the fabric. This helps to strengthen the border edges.

Your first thread on fine linen will invariably be a b★★★★r! If it snaps, don't panic – you can always weave the end in.

Continue in this way, drawing parallel threads until the borders are as wide as you require. Before beginning the stitchwork do match the thread to the fabric. For instance, on fine linen use a reel cotton; coarser fabrics require heavier thread.

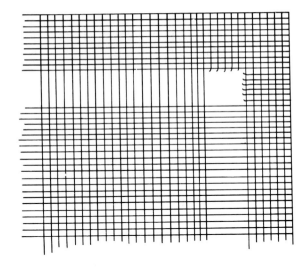

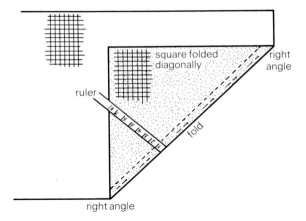

Cutting on the cross

Fabric cut on the cross-weave has a more elastic quality than straight-grain cutting. It is invaluable for rouleaux, facings and bindings, especially where they have to follow a curve.

The first step is to find the cross of the material. Work with the selvedge, or a straight edge, and using a few pins, mark out a square. Fold it diagonally (the length of the diagonal will be your longest strip).

If you need more than one strip of material, cut additional strips across the diagonal from both the top and bottom triangles of fabric. To prevent the fabric from slipping, pin before cutting.

In the projects, I have avoided joining strips cut on the cross, as even a perfect join on a collar or dress neckline would look out of place.

To sidestep any complications I attached the piping around the cushions with a simple, straight join. However, it may be necessary to join on the cross if you need a lot of piping. This is an easy method:

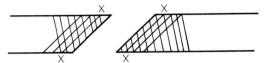

Pick out on your material the longer lines of thread and mark them lightly. I have indicated these with an X.

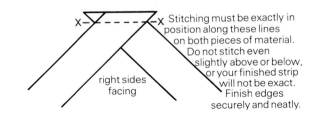

Stitching must be exactly in position along these lines on both pieces of material. Do not stitch even slightly above or below, or your finished strip will not be exact. Finish edges securely and neatly.

Don't keep those pictures locked away. Even your earliest attempts can look quite professional once framed and hung as part of a displayed collection.

Picture It

If you have never sketched since you were at school, it's high time you took it up again. Embroidery and design go hand in hand, and it really does not matter whether or not you can draw.

Keep a sketchbook handy and have a go. I have a little black sketch-pad the same size as my pocket stitch books. Inspiration is everywhere and you can only get better and better.

If you prefer, you could at first enlist an artistic friend, or use transfers, for your designs while you put in some practice. Never be self-conscious about your efforts. Sketching is not photography, and most of my pictures are done in a very simple, naive style.

I was once stuck in my Mini in a traffic jam watching an old man behind the wheel of his lorry. He was a picture of perfect contentment with his little dog – both of them smiling – and his transistor radio hanging up.

I made a lightning sketch of him and later turned it into an embroidery picture. My father framed it for me, and years later I am still quite proud of the wing mirrors.

An artist friend of mine says: 'If you have done a picture – hang it up; if you've made a cushion, put it out.'

Only by hanging your pictures can you think: I'll do better than that next time. As you improve, take it down and put another up.

Occasionally I have made individual pictures for friends. One is a kindly caricature of a friend who loves cooking. I embroidered him with a little pot tummy, sampling food from a ladle.

Another is of my eighteen-year-old son lying on a sofa – he is 6 ft 3 in and all legs, and can really never get comfortable. At first I thought it was terrific – exactly what I wanted to achieve. Later I bundled it away because it seemed out of proportion and I was a little ashamed of it. Recently I took it out again, and I now feel it's not so bad. After all, it was not meant to be a perfect likeness. It was exactly as I saw him at the time. The sofa was weeny and he really did seem all quiff and legs. It is rather like a child's eye view.

It is a nice idea to embroider a picture of your house. I have one, which is rather gaudy, of a little cottage I bought in Surrey.

Needlework, as an art of the hands, is relaxing, and I find that sketching work plans has the same effect.

I like to mix mediums whenever I can. Fabric paints and inks can be used for lettering as a contrast to the texture of the stitchwork. Always check if the paint you intend to use is washable, although on pictures behind glass the problem seldom arises.

Try to use your own lettering whenever you can. Even if your script is not particularly neat, at least it is yours and gives an authentic touch.

Nearly all my pictures are embroidered, though I worked the Biba motif in tapestry work because it fitted their Deco style so well. It is in memory of Biba, because I was so smitten by the shop and full of admiration for Barbara Hulanicki, who was such an innovator.

Usually I find tapestry work a little tedious, but I wanted to add it to my repertoire. My motto is 'have a go'; it is the only way to find what suits you best.

Small pictures are inexpensive to make, especially if you hoard your linen scraps and have an assortment of silks to hand. All of mine are tiny and, although the writing may sometimes be clumsy or a circle slightly imperfect, I don't believe it really matters. It is a great confidence-booster to visit museums and examine fine examples of needlework. Quite often you can spot mistakes, or even pieces that have been missed out altogether.

When you work out the size of your picture, always add a couple of inches all round to turn over onto a hardboard mount for framing. This keeps your masterpiece taut and unwrinkled.

Despite anyone who says otherwise, it is perfectly all right to stitch all over the place on the wrong side of a picture. It will not be seen when it is finished; unlike, say, a table-cloth where it is worth taking the trouble to be neat on the reverse.

THE SADDLE-BACK PIG

My brother-in-law has a rare-breeds farm park in the Cotswolds and we have had some happy times there. Visits are a rare occasion, when I have time on my hands to sit in the fields and draw the animals.

This particular sow had recently farrowed and was sporting a set of extremely sore nipples from her hungry offspring. I felt quite sorry for her! I immortalized her mostly in long and short stitch, set at different angles to create shade and rolls of rippling bacon.

If you have an affinity for saddle-back pigs in a delicate condition, begin by tracing the design outline onto clean paper. Lay out your linen – it should be about 11 in sq – on a flat surface. I used a coarse, rustic texture, almost the colour of sacking. Transfer the outline to the fabric using carbon paper, remembering to lift the paper to ensure you have not missed anything out.

Hold the linen in a ring frame so your freestyle embroidery will maintain an even tension.

THE JACOB RAM

My Jacob Ram was also sketched in the Cotswolds. I find my drawings improve with each visit – or perhaps the animals are subtly changing shape.

This ram was quite easy because he is just a mass of French knots. This, incidentally, is also a good technique for embroidering children with those knobbly hairstyles.

If you feel you can draw sheep better than I can, I urge you to have a go.

I embroidered mine on an 8 in frame, and used shading here and there on the pink, cream and grey from my bundle of odd threads and snippets.

When you cover the face in long and short stitch, work the features in later. Take care, because setting each stitch can be tricky – one false move and you change the whole expression.

When making a picture inside a circle, outline your circle first. I drew around a china strawberry bowl, as it was nearest to the size I wanted. Space the lettering carefully to make sure you can fit it all in. Then I transferred my sketch to the fabric, centring it in the circle of lettering.

Opposite
The saddle-back pig.

Jacob Ram stitch key

Face	*long and short stitch*	white with some pink shading
Eyes	*satin stitch*	black
Lashes	*straight stitch*	white
Eye surround	*long and short stitch*	pale pink
Nose and mouth	*split stitch*	black
Ears	*long and short stitch*	pale pink edged with white
Section 1	*French knots*	butter
Section 2	*French knots*	pale cream, grey at edges
Section 3	*long and short stitch*	dark to mid brown
Section 4	*French knots*	cream
Section 5	*French knots*	cream with a touch of grey
Legs	*long and short or close stem stitch*	black
Horns a	*satin stitch*	grey
Horns b	*satin stitch*	coffee
Horns c	*satin stitch*	cream
Horns d	*satin stitch*	dark brown
Horns e	*satin stitch*	mid brown
Circle	*split stitch*	black
Lettering	*split stitch*	black

The Jacob Ram.

Happy visits to my brother-in-law's rare-breeds farm park in the Cotswolds have been immortalized in my embroidered sketch-pictures of the saddle-back pig and the Jacob Ram.

Home sweet home.

HOME SWEET HOME

I always wanted to make my own version of those beautiful samplers found dotted around antique shops and country houses.

As well as providing a good grounding in the basics of needlework, they were used to teach children to spell and count. Behind their simplicity there is an intriguing air of mystery about who made them, what sort of lives they led, and who did they marry? All their thoughts as they sewed are tied up in each stitch.

Samplers were my first venture in working in wool. Because I admire so much the work of needlewomen of years gone by, I chose faded shades of blue and pink for an authentic touch.

If you attempt one, do try to use a frame to prevent a 'pulled' look on your finished work. Your fabric can be pinned to an old wooden picture frame as a substitute for an embroidery frame, if necessary.

What you need
A 10 in sq piece of tapestry base fabric, and tapestry wools in soft, dusty shades of dark pink, paler pink and blue. The little blue flowers have a hint of yellow and a single black dot in the centre.

Lettering
Work out the spacing of the words on a 7 in sq piece of paper – graph paper makes the job easier – and transfer this onto the canvas using carbon.

How to make it
The picture itself is 8 in sq, but mark out a 7 in square on your pattern paper. This leaves a $\frac{1}{2}$ in border all round, which is covered in a dark pink *Gros Point stitch*. It sounds grand, but it is really just a half cross stitch.

I worked the sampler row by row from the top. If you find the colour changes confusing, shade them in on your pattern paper as a guide.

In Gros Point the stitches are slanted on the right side and vertical on the wrong side. So the first row of your border goes:

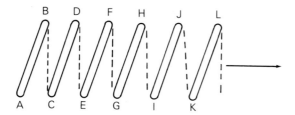

The thread comes through at A and is inserted at B, out again at C and into D, and so on. When you reach the end, the second row is worked right to left:

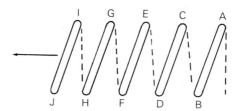

This time, stitch from top to bottom, slanting it in the same direction as the first row, and keeping the stitches on the wrong side vertical. The beauty of Gros Point lies in its symmetry which, in turn, depends upon an even tension.

Within the border the whole of the sampler background is worked in cream *Gros Point filling stitch*. This should be added, row by row, as you do the lettering.

The hearts and flowers are embroidered in *Petit Point stitch*, sometimes known as *tent stitch*, which is very fine and perfect for detail, even on tiny designs.

The stitch slants a little on the right side, and has a greater angle on the wrong side. Work from right to left, bringing the thread out at the bottom of the stitch and in at the top:

Then back in the opposite direction for the next row, with the thread emerging at the top of the stitch and inserted at the bottom:

As in its larger version, Gros Point, care must be taken to maintain an even tension.

When the stitchwork is complete, lay the fabric on a soft pad, cover, and press on the reverse.

Framing

Mount your work by stitching it firmly around an 8 in sq of hardboard with strong thread. Lace the back with vertical and horizontal stitches, checking periodically that your needlework has not been pulled out of shape.

Eight inch frames for your finished sampler can be bought in most department stores.

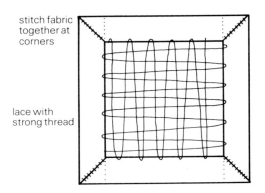

stitch fabric together at corners

lace with strong thread

My long-legged son. Not a perfect likeness maybe, but a very special memory nevertheless.

Bags of Fun

Just like a picture, every cushion tells a story. I can remember working on each one I have made. Some began with patterns that happened to catch my eye, others I designed as mementoes of holidays and friends.

I began making cushions to heap on a favourite old sofa, so I kept them to a practical size. My needlework motto is: think small. Stitchwork tends to become lost on a large area. As needlework cushions are floppy anyway, they need a small, firm base.

If you prefer them bigger, tapestry work is more suitable because it is heavier and helps the cushion hold its shape. Unfortunately, like the 'Egg Plant That Ate Chicago', they can take over the house.

Cushion-making is ideal for anyone itching to have a go at something beautiful and useful. You can pile up your work and show it off. Or – as in my case – see where you went wrong and vow to improve on it next time! Needlework is rewarding but it tends to gnaw away at you, spurring you on to better things. So be warned!

A useful piece of cushion equipment is a tin of tiny beads; I keep one in my sewing basket and dip into it to enhance my freestyle embroidery. Over the years I have bought and begged so many beads that it is almost full to the brim. Beads are a marvellous source of inspiration for those finishing touches, so jackdaw habits, I suppose, do have their uses.

At first I used transfer embroidery designs, but as I progressed I copied in pencil just the parts which caught my fancy. Now I have moved on a little and draw my own designs.

One, for instance, is a picture of my children gazing at the crib and candles when we visited Bethlehem. Another cushion has a picture of a table laid with lurid red napkins and plates, drawn by an artist friend. I keep it as an amusing reminder of a holiday years ago when friends tried their hand at matchmaking us. They insisted on ordering countless teas-for-two as we sat at the dreaded table grimacing.

In the corner of the cushion, I stitched my initials and the date, as I do on all my work.

Try to use natural fabrics whenever you can. If necessary, put off your project and save up for a piece of good linen or heavy cotton, otherwise your work will be wasted.

Sometimes I put cushions away for a year or two before bringing them out again or giving them to my children. If I had used man-made fabric they simply would not survive. Incidentally, do not worry about pale, natural colours – I have found they remain surprisingly clean.

Feather-filled cushion bases can be bought in all shapes and sizes in most department stores. Take it from me: there is no easy way to fill your own cushion without the house looking as though it has been struck by a blizzard.

To save money you can run two rows of machine stitching across an old feather pillow and cut it in half.

For finishing, I prefer not to use bulky zips. Instead I oversew one edge of the cushion, which can easily be unpicked and restitched after laundering.

EMBROIDERED CUSHION

This is one of a set of cushions I made for the family sofa. I discovered the design in a German picture book and copied it to add to my collection. Later I adapted it to suit the fabric and stitchwork I had in mind.

It took a long pencil and a large rubber to achieve the result I was looking for. I wanted to accentuate the central theme without overloading the cover and making it 'fussy'. Cushions, after all, are for relaxing on, and a wise scattering of plain surfaces rests easy on the eye.

The thorny problem, as always, is transferring your masterpiece onto the fabric. Copying it directly in freehand by pencil is an anxious business, for which the only cure is practice. So do go lightly in soft pencil – the final outline can always be darkened later.

There is, however, a simpler method for which you need only a piece of carbon paper and a smooth surface that you are prepared to stick drawing pins into.

Pin down your fabric and place your paper design over it in the right position. Then pin down the paper too – but only along one edge, to make a hinge. This allows you to lift and place the carbon, face down, between them. (Don't forget to ensure that it is big enough to cover the whole design!) If black is too bold for what you have in mind, office suppliers stock carbons in several other colours.

Now you can go over the design in hard pencil, pressing firmly if the material is coarse. If the fabric is fine, use a sharp pencil for a delicate line, holding the 'sandwich' firmly to prevent it slipping.

When you have finished, raise one side of the paper to make absolutely sure nothing has been left out. To fix the design, and prevent the carbon outline smudging, remove it from the board, cover with clean tissue paper and simply press with a warm iron.

What you need

My filled cushion base was 12 in square. To cover it I needed about $1\frac{1}{3}$ yd of 36 in wide fabric. Ask if it is pre-shrunk – if not, add a little to the size you are buying and wash and press it before starting. The shade I chose was almond, in a coarse natural cotton which washes well and lasts almost for ever.

The silks were the same colour, varying slightly in shade. I also picked out a few tiny wooden beads to highlight the fabric grain and raised stitchwork.

The cushion takes $1\frac{1}{2}$ yd of piping cord. I covered mine in the same fabric but, if you wish to try something different, ready-covered piping cord can be obtained by the yard in contrasting or complementary colours.

If you really want to splash out there are shops which will pipe your cushions beautifully to order.

Measuring up

For a 12×12 in cushion, cut two paper patterns – for back and front – each 13×13 in. Smooth out your fabric and pin them to it:

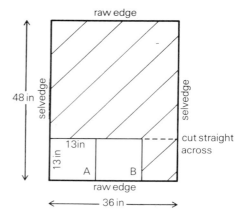

Cutting out

I have allowed for small, neat seams, so mark the fabric carefully with a pencil before you cut.

Place pieces A and B face to face and, using a 10p coin as a template, round off the corners and trim. They can now be put to one side while you concentrate on the piping.

That leftover corner piece can be squirrelled away for another occasion. I hoard scraps to use later for small brooch cushions, pin cushions and pictures. To a fully-fledged embroidery junkie, even the tiniest piece is a new challenge.

Piping

If you feel adventurous enough to try it yourself, the remaining piece of fabric (35×36 in) can be used to trim your cushion with only one join.

Piping is always cut on the cross-weave to give elasticity and to allow the material to follow curved edges and shapes.

First draw a line 1 in from the edge, down the 36 in width, and trim off to obtain a 35 in square.

Now fold the fabric diagonally, inserting a few pins to hold it in position. Along the fold, mark a line 1 in from the edge, and trim:

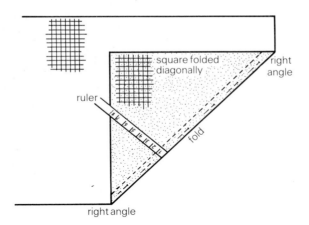

This gives a 2 in wide cross-weave strip to cover the piping cord. Fold the piping cord into the fabric, pin the edges together, and use a small *running stitch* to ensure a snug fit. Each end should then be squarely trimmed.

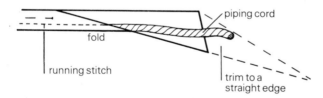

Making up

I piped the back of the cushion cover first, leaving the front panel free for embroidery. Smooth out the back fabric and, pinning as you go, join together the raw edges of the piping strip and the cushion:

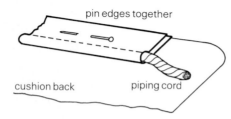

Work your way right round the cover, back to the beginning. Incidentally, for an unobtrusive finish always try to start away from a corner.

To bring the two ends of the piping together with the correct cross-weave join requires quite a lot of needlework experience. But, by using a butt join you can neatly sidestep an unwelcome headache.

Trim the fabric piping cover, leaving just enough material for a small join. The cord should be trimmed back slightly further than the fabric, so that the ends barely meet, to avoid unsightly knobbles.

Now spread open the piping covers and *backstitch* the ends firmly together on the wrong side:

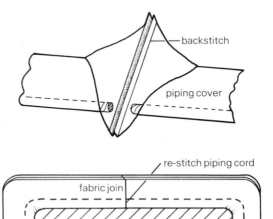

The cover is folded back over the piping cord and joined by continuing the original running stitch. It can now be pinned into place on the cushion cover.

With that out of the way, the piping trim can finally be attached to the cover with running stitch, following the same line of stitchwork as was used to secure the piping cord.

The back of the cushion is now complete.

Front cover

The embroidery is framed by a double line of drawn threadwork. Picking out individual threads needs a strong light and a steady hand. It is not a task to be tackled in a hurry – so whiz through the housework to allow yourself plenty of time.

There was a period when housewives used drawn threadwork extensively on their household linen. Today it has become, sadly, something of a lost art. Although it requires precision, there is a pleasing logical progress about it which gives the finished piece a lovely, timeless quality.

It is, however, very fine work and periods set aside for it should not be too prolonged. But do have a go – it never fails to impress and will do wonders for your reputation as a needlewoman!

Opposite *Embroidered cushions made with natural fabrics can be both beautiful and useful.*

Right *For the front cushion-cover embroidery I used a design I had discovered in a German picture book, and adapted it to suit the fabric and stitchwork. I keep a file of designs, so that I can use them again. This design was also used for the front embroidery on the yellow gingham smock dress.*

Drawing threads

Measure a margin of approximately $2\frac{1}{2}$ in on each side of the front cover, and mark out an inner square.

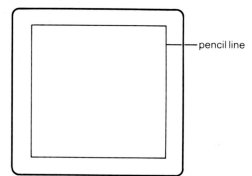
pencil line

Somewhere in the middle of the pencil line running *across* the fabric (not vertically) use your needle to pick out a thread. Pull it up gently and snip. Now draw out each piece of the thread towards the pencil corners to your right and left. Remove four or five adjoining parallel threads in the same way:

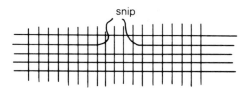
snip

Take one of the strands, thread it onto your needle, and weave it into the outer edge of the cover. Snip off the surplus on the underside. Repeat with the remaining loose threads to give a tightly-darned corner at each end.

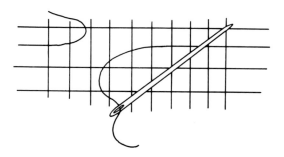

One side of the frame is now complete. Continue by drawing the same number of threads on the remaining three sides of the rectangle. As you progress, turn each section to the top, so that you are always working in the same direction and avoid snipping the wrong threads. The finished corners should now be quite firm to resist wear and tear on your cushion:

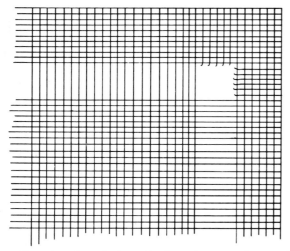

Now for the stitchwork. A variety can be used on drawn threads, but perhaps the simplest is *ladder hemstitch*, which gives an attractive finish.

Thread your needle with a couple of strands of silk – not too long, as the thread wears as you sew. The correct number of strands depends on the weight of your fabric, so have a test run on a scrap of fabric if you think you may need more or less.

Choose a corner to begin at, working right to left if you are right-handed – the opposite way if you are left-handed.

Bring the needle up about two threads beneath the lowest drawn thread. Pass it behind four loose vertical threads, drawing the silk through. Then insert the needle behind the same threads, bringing it out two threads down, in line with your starting point:

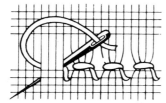

Continue the stitch right around the square. Then repeat along the upper edge of the drawn thread:

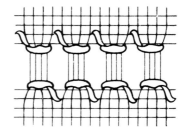

Ladder hemstitch is quite relaxing once you get into the swing of it – and pretty unbeatable for silencing anyone with the irritating habit of picking up other people's stitchwork.

If you enjoyed doing it (and contrary to some dour opinion, fun *is* permissible in needlework) you might wish to spread your wings a little. Add another square – 1 in outside the first – and try your hand at *zigzag hemstitch*.

You will need to draw out slightly more threads to create an open effect, again darning each one back into the corners for firmness. Zigzag is similar to ladder hemstitch, so you will be working your way around one side of the drawn threads as before, only this time pass the needle behind six loose threads instead of four.

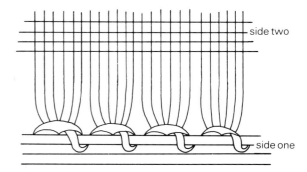

side two

side one

For the second side, the threads in each group of six are divided in half. To start side two, pick up half the first group of six vertical threads, pass the needle behind them and draw it out.

Now pass again behind the same threads and finish the movement by inserting the needle two threads down into the fabric, and pull through.

For the next stitch pass the needle behind the remaining three threads of the first group *and* the first three of the next cluster. Then simply continue, repeating the pattern. It is fairly easy once the penny drops. Zigzag and ladder hemstitch can be used with great effect on a variety of embroidery designs.

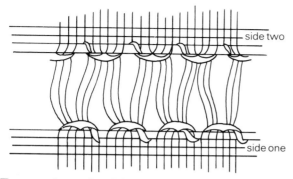

Free-style embroidery

All that painstaking drawn threadwork is a fitting framework for a beautiful embroidered centre-piece. It is important to draw or transfer something that centres well inside the hemstitch bordering.

If you decide to use my design, trace it first; then, using the carbon paper method, transfer it to the fabric – remembering to fix the print by pressing with a warm iron and tissue paper.

First of all, however, it is a good idea to work out which stitches you plan to use, and where you intend to place your beads for the best effect.

For the embroidery I used a round frame, about 6 in in diameter. If you have not used one before, try investing in a small selection of different sizes – they make the job so much easier and give the stitchwork a tighter, more professional look. Do be careful not to catch the corners of your drawn threadwork in the frame when tightening it up.

Overcast stitch

This is sometimes known as *trailing stitch* because threads are trailed over the outline of the design before being oversewn. A simpler method is to

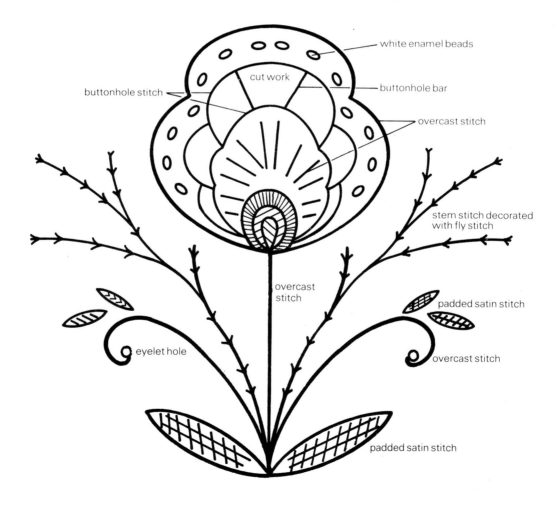

follow the line with running stitch. This, in the same way, is then overcast with small, closely-set satin stitches. I call it *cord stitch* because of its finished appearance, and I have used it for so long I can't remember where I picked it up. To add to the confusion, it quite possibly has a proper name. Anyway, it works beautifully – so who cares?

Whichever you choose – trailing thread or running stitch – begin by bringing up two threads at the starting point, making sure they are long enough to cover the whole of the outline you plan to sew *plus* about 6 in to finish off. Re-thread the needle with three threads of silk, and bring it through at the starting point. If you are doing trailing stitch, hold down the loose-laid threads on the outline with your thumb and work small satin stitches closely over them. When you come to the end of the design finish off by passing the laid threads through to the back of the work.

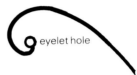

eyelet hole

Eyelet holes
I think of these as the full-stops and commas of needlework. They help to bring embroidery to life and give it an appealing sense of order. Work a row of small *running stitches* round the circle, and

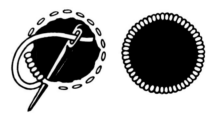

pierce the centre with a stiletto. If you are left with any ragged edges, fold them to the back. Sew over both the edge and the running stitch using *overcast stitch* and finish off at the back of the work.

Satin stitch
This is simple, but eye-catching and effective. Satin stitch is worked with straight stitches across the shape of the design. Keep them as close

running stitch

padded satin stitch

together as you possibly can, and take care to make a neat edge. To give your work a little body, try filling in the outline with running stitches first, then lay the satin stitch over them.

Stem stitch
Before attempting the stems, work the tiny 'V' decorations in *fly stitch*. Bring up your thread on the top left-hand side of the 'V'. Leave a loop and insert the needle at the top right side, coming out again at the bottom of the 'V' to tie down the loop with a small stitch.

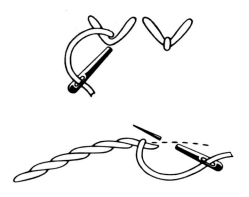

Stem stitch itself gives a binding effect – but always work from left to right, keeping the loose thread on the right-hand side of the needle as you go.

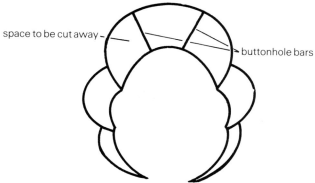

space to be cut away

buttonhole bars

Cut work
If, up to this point, the embroidery has been very demanding, and the dishes are piling up, the rest of the design can be finished by following the outline in *overcast stitch*, or *cord stitch* as I call it.

On the other hand, the blood may be coursing and you may have developed a thirst for new frontiers.

This then is the time to step out and try your hand at cut work. It isn't too difficult, but it requires a little time, a degree of precision and a large helping of patience.

The idea is to bind the edges of the motif with simple *buttonhole stitch*, and later to cut away the space in between. However, because it is such an odd shape, it is necessary to make supports with *buttonhole bars*, rather like beams holding a building together.

The rule of cut work is to always begin with your stitch-bars, so that you have a firm foundation ready to tie your work in position for the final cutting. Always use an embroidery frame for cut work – without one it will prove as difficult as trying to tap dance in your stocking feet – and the bars will not have the right tension.

To work the bars take a single thread across the space and back again. Secure it with a small stitch, then buttonhole stitch closely over the loose bars you have made, taking care not to pick up any fabric.

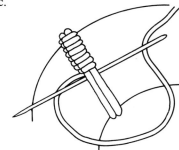

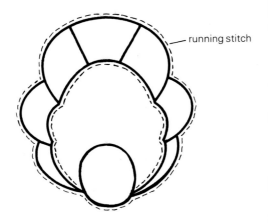

running stitch

Next the outline of the design should be followed with a small running stitch to prepare for the buttonholing.

Remember: the buttonhole stitch should cover the running stitch completely, and make as neat an edge as possible.

With the stitch-bars and buttonholing out of the way, the centre-pieces can now be cut out. Take a lot of care over this. Use small, sharp scissors and don't worry about any little threads that may stick out and give it a frayed look. These can be snipped off after the first laundering. Do, however, take special care when cutting away beneath the bars that hold the work in shape.

Now for the finishing touches. Choose the size and colour of your beads and arrange them sparingly. If they are very small you will need a beading needle to thread them, securing them with a couple of tiny stitches on the underside.

If, as I did, you are making a set of cushions, vary each one slightly while keeping to the same size, colour and basic design.

Assembling the cushion

Press the pieces carefully on the wrong side before putting them together. Smooth down the cushion back with the right side and piping uppermost. Place the cushion front panel, face down, on top of it and pin the edges together into position.

With the cushion completely inside out, *backstitch* round three sides over the original *running*

stitch used on the piping. Turn the cover the right way out and stuff with your feather inner cushion. To finish off oversew the opening neatly.

BROOCH CUSHION

Brooch cushions were once a familiar sight in Edwardian boudoirs, and I think it's high time they enjoyed a comeback. If you have a penchant for brooches or hat-pins, a tiny cushion could look lovely on your dressing-table to display your collection.

I keep mine on a table at my bedside. Despite its size it makes its own contribution to the atmosphere of the room. Later we shall take a closer look at hand-worked bed linen and table coverings. Even small, delicately-embroidered items can add so much to the style of your boudoir; sorry, bedroom. Needlework, especially in the firelight, has a timeless quality that is becoming more elusive in today's hi-tech world.

When I set out to make my first brooch cushion, I suppose I had in mind all the pretty examples I had seen in antique shops around the country.

I cut up an old sheet for the fabric but, on reflection, I am not too sure it was a good idea. It had seen better days and might not wear as long as I had hoped. But, like everything else in stitchwork, I learn as I go along.

It is one of my favourite pieces yet, when I take a long, hard look at it, perhaps a little clumsy. When I see mistakes in my work I have to suppress a great urge to bundle the lot under my jumper out of sight. One day the ultimate piece in all its pristine perfection will be created – and I'll possibly become rapidly fed up with it.

Brooch cushions, however, do have one appealing feature – they cost next to nothing to make. Mine, for instance, was completely put together from scraps.

What you need

If you are making the cushion from new fabric you will require two 9 in squares of fine handkerchief-weight linen. Indeed, a pair of men's handkerchiefs would do nicely. Every household must have at least one unopened box from Auntie Flo that's been lying around since last Christmas.

Incidentally, when you trim the fabric to size, cut along the grain of the linen, as this will keep the lines of drawn threadwork both parallel and straight.

You will need two 5 in squares of flesh-coloured

jap silk (I recycled scraps from a piece I used to repair an antique blouse).

You will also need a selection of white embroidery silks, a few translucent beads and a sheet of white paper to make the pattern. A sharp pencil will come in handy too!

For the cushion filling you could buy a small quantity of washable padding. To keep it inexpensive I cut a pair of white tights into tiny pieces – any other colour will run in the wash and ruin everything.

Here's how
Begin by marking out a square, 2 in in from the edge, on both the front and back pieces of the cushion: square A in the diagram. This will be used later for joining up the back and front.

Now take the front only and draw in two more squares. B is $\frac{1}{2}$ in smaller than A; and C is $\frac{1}{2}$ in smaller than B:

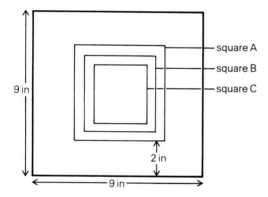

Squares B and C are for drawn threadwork.

I decided to begin by working on the centre-piece, using a transfer from the Royal School of Needlework. As the project was so small and detailed, I used my magnifying glass and a small ring frame.

If you wish to embroider a design similar to the one I chose, the pattern below is the right size to be transferred directly to the centre square. Trace it first, then transfer it to the fabric using carbon paper and a sharp pencil. The method is described in detail in the first cushion project (page 33).

Embroidery
Four flower heads and the bow are worked in *padded satin stitch*. The padding is made with a small running stitch. Satin stitch is then laid over the top. Take care to keep the tension even and aim for a neat edge round the outline.

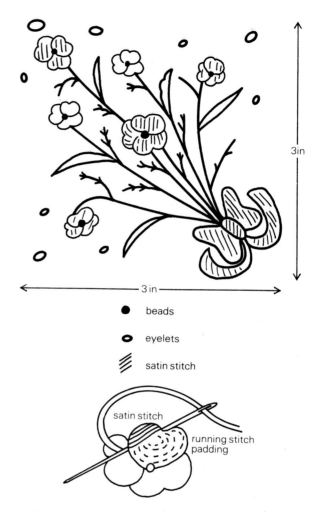

●	beads
⬭	eyelets
▨	satin stitch

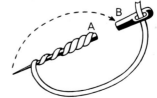

The other flowers are simply outlined in *overcast* or *cord stitch*. Follow the shape in small *running stitch*, then work over it with a close satin stitch. Step-by-step instructions can be found in the cushion project (pages 33–5).

Flower stems are done in *cord stitch*, decorated at intervals with two straight stitches shaped in a 'V'.

The leaves are *bullion knots* – one knot is enough for each, but you can use two side by side if you wish. It is one of my favourite stitches, effective yet easy to work:

Secure your thread at the back of the work and bring through at point A. Then insert the needle at B, allowing it to protrude at A. Twist the thread round and round the needle until you have enough coils to cover the space between A and B. Now, holding the coils lightly with your left thumb, draw the needle through them and insert it back into point B. This will lay the bullion knot flat between A and B, and you can finish off on the underside.

Eyelet holes
Work a circle of minute *running stitches* around the eyelet hole outline – the magnifying glass is a boon here – then pierce the centre and fold back any ragged edges. Closely oversew the folded edge all around, trimming off any tatty pieces on the blind side later.

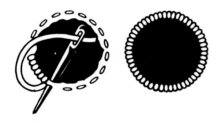

The final task is to select some beads – use a beading needle if they are very small – and secure them tightly in the flower centres.

The embroidery now only needs removing from the frame and a swift press on the wrong side.

Drawn threadwork
Always allow yourself plenty of time for drawn threadwork, even if you have to insist that the family fend for themselves for a couple of hours.

Because of the size of the brooch cushion, a magnifying glass – the type that hangs round your neck, leaving both hands free – is an enormous help.

Fasten the fabric in your embroidery frame and begin in the middle of one of the sides of square B. Always work on a horizontal line to avoid confusing the warp and weft of the linen.

Again, a detailed guide to drawn threadwork can be found in the cushion project (pages 31–3). As a refresher, select a thread, lift it gently with the point of your needle, and snip. Then draw out each half, a section at a time, to the right and left corners of the square. When they are completely free, thread one of them onto your needle and darn it back into the corner, finishing on the wrong side of the fabric.

Draw about five parallel threads in this way, then turn the square to work horizontally along the next side.

Use one of the *hemstitch* variations on your border. For square C, draw the threads in the same way, but try a different style of hemstitch.

If, for instance, you choose *ladder hemstitch* for square B, you could repeat the stitch on square C, but bind the centres of the bars in groups of three with a single strand of machine cotton to give a star effect. Press the work with a warm iron when complete.

Padding
Now for the little pad of jap silk. *Backstitch* the pieces together on three sides and turn right-side out. Stuff the bag with your padding, or chopped-up white tights, taking care not to overfill. Close by *hemstitching* the opening.

By this time the whole thing is looking more like a cushion. Place the pad between the linen covers (right sides facing outwards) then pin and tack into position, following the line of square A, marked on both sides of the cover.

To secure the pad sew around the line of square A with two or three layers of *running stitch* to give it strength, and remove the tacking. To finish off, cover the running stitch with a tiny, close-set *satin stitch*:

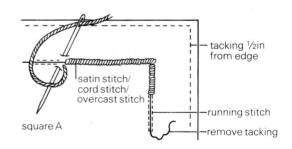

Scalloping
The work took just a few evenings to do before I was ready for the scalloped edges. To prepare for them, tack around the outer edge of the cushion, about $\frac{1}{2}$ in from the edge.

I drew the scallops freehand but, if that worries you, it is possible to buy scalloping transfers. Mine are slightly uneven, so if you plan to draw your own, try to make them as symmetrical as possible. It is easier if you start in a corner.

Working on your 9 in sq paper pattern, pencil in

*A delicately-embroidered brooch cushion costs next to nothing to
make and yet it can completely transform your dressing-table*

square A to make a 2 in border. This is the baseline for your scallops, which can be drawn using a 5p or 2p coin; or each alternately if you prefer an up-and-down effect.

Perhaps the most important piece of equipment at this stage is a rubber. Persevere until you get one line of scalloping right, then cut it out and fold and re-fold the paper as a pattern for the remaining three sides.

When you are satisfied, lay your cut-out scallop pattern over the linen pad and pin down:

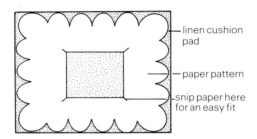

— linen cushion pad

— paper pattern

— snip paper here for an easy fit

Draw round the scallops on the linen, then remove the pattern paper and add an inner guideline for the embroidery:

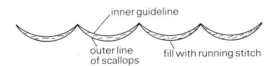

inner guideline

outer line of scallops

fill with running stitch

The scallops can now be filled with *running stitch* to bind together the two layers of fabric, and provide body for the buttonholing.

Do not cut the scallops yet, They must first be worked all around in *buttonhole stitch*. I suggest using two threads from the skein, quite short in length to prevent them fraying on the needle eye.

When the stitching is complete, the raw edge of the scallops can finally be cut away. On the other hand, you may wish to cut as you go: embroidering three scallops, cutting the first two, and so on. Any loose, hanging threads can be trimmed later.

Eyelets

When I examine my brooch cushion closely, I think I used too thick a thread on the eyelet holes. Try to avoid the same mistake.

The original tacking just below the scalloping can be removed and the position of the eyelet holes marked on the fabric. There are countless combinations to choose from:

When you have laid out your design, bind and pierce the eyelets as you did in the freestyle embroidery. They can also be interspersed with small flowers made from *double cross stitch* and decorated with leftover beads.

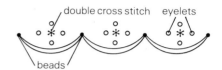

double cross stitch   eyelets

beads

The brooch cushion is now ready for your dressing-table – and don't forget to sign your work after all that effort!

PIN CUSHION

Here is an idea for using up odd scraps to make a delicate pin cushion or scented sachet. It costs only time and a little dedication. The embroidery stitches are fairly simple – the most demanding aspect is the tiny detail of the needlework.

Use a magnifying glass throughout, if you can. Ultimately it will save time, eyestrain and more than a few mistakes. The result is creatively very satisfying, certainly eye-catching, and guaranteed to set off your work-box superbly.

What you need
Two 5 in circles of white or cream linen.
Cream or white silks, and pale green silks for the leaves.
Two 3 in circles of pale green silk or cotton.
A selection of tiny, colourless and clear-green beads.
A pair of old white tights to cut into small scraps, *or* a little white padding, *or* a handful of crushed pot pourri.

How to make it
Place the two 3 in silk circles back to back, and stitch around the outside, leaving a $1\frac{1}{2}$ in gap. Turn right-side out, fill, and oversew the opening.

Take one of the 5 in linen circles and, using carbon paper, transfer the design below. Remember, there will be an outer rim of linen to be trimmed away after buttonholing circle A.

This edge also means that you can use a 4 in circular frame for the centre embroidery.

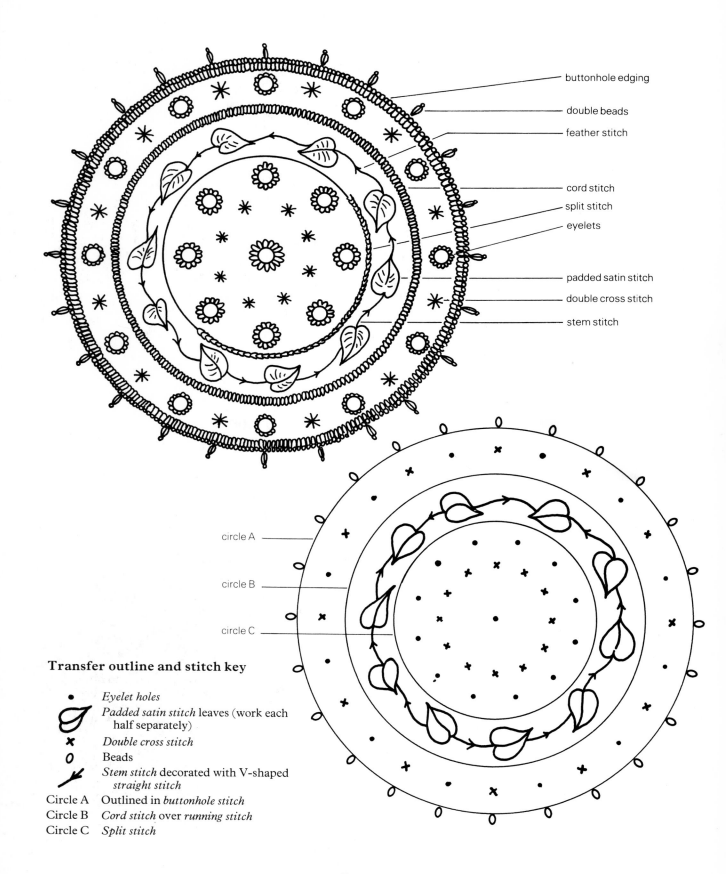

buttonhole edging

double beads

feather stitch

cord stitch

split stitch

eyelets

padded satin stitch

double cross stitch

stem stitch

circle A

circle B

circle C

Transfer outline and stitch key

- •   *Eyelet holes*
- *Padded satin stitch* leaves (work each half separately)
- ✗   *Double cross stitch*
- 0   Beads
- *Stem stitch* decorated with V-shaped straight stitch

Circle A   Outlined in *buttonhole stitch*
Circle B   *Cord stitch* over *running stitch*
Circle C   *Split stitch*

You can make a unique set of cushion covers for the living-room, embroidered with caricatures of your family. Any left-over scraps can be made into a pin cushion, like the lace-trimmed one, with the red flower embroidery design, in this photograph.

Free-style embroidery

With your fabric set in the frame, embroider around circle C in *split stitch*. Then begin the centre circle eyelets, alternating with *double cross stitch*, and finishing on the single eyelet in the centre.

The leaves are worked in *padded satin stitch* (on a *running stitch* foundation). When you have completed this, stitch in the decorative 'V's in *straight stitch* before joining each leaf with *stem stitch*.

Finally, work the eyelets and *double cross stitch* between circles A and B. A tiny translucent green bead in the centre of each cross stitch gives a pretty effect.

Remove the embroidery from the frame and press on the wrong side.

Assembly

Lay the silk pad in the centre of the back linen circle and cover it with the top section. The right side of the embroidery should be uppermost.

Pin together the back and front covers along the line of circle B to enclose the silk pad. Then make two rows of *running stitch* along the line of circle B. Finish this off with *cord stitch*, closely oversewing the running stitch.

Tack around the raw edge of the covers to hold both sides together. When they are secure, work the eyelets and *double cross stitch* between circles A and B.

Stitch around the outline of circle A with a small, firm running stitch, and cover the completed running stitch with close *buttonholing*. The raw edge can now be trimmed away.

Attach the beads with small stitches, taking care to conceal them in the close-set buttonholing.

Result: a miniature masterpiece.

Faggoting

Faggoting means joining together two pieces of fabric, leaving a gap between them, using *insertion stitch*.

It is sad that faggoting has become neglected today because the finished effect is so beautiful.

I made myself a grey-and-white pinstripe, lawn tunic blouse with a faggoted neckline, and continued the theme by joining on the sleeves with insertion stitch.

This technique is easy to try on a basic blouse made up from a pattern. A suitable style should have a plain, round neckline and a straight, slit-type back opening. Remember: when you buy the fabric for the blouse you will need an extra yard for the faggoting.

If you fancy having a go at joining the sleeves with insertion stitch, too, be sure that the pattern has straight, off-the-shoulder seams like mine.

On the other hand, if this is your first attempt at faggoting, and insertion stitch is as familiar to you as the Theory of Relativity, it may be better just to concentrate on the neckline. Decorative sleeve seams can be left for another day; in which case, you would simply make up the blouse, following your pattern instructions for sewing the basics and setting in the sleeves. Leave the neckline and back opening ready for the faggoting.

I chose my pinstripe fabric while browsing in Liberty, and bought a very plain pattern which looked easily adaptable for what I had in mind.

French knots decorate
the facing here
on the top rouleaux

4 rouleaux joined by
twisted insertion stitch

sleeves joined
with twisted
insertion stitch

Cutting the neckline

The first step is to scoop the neckline ready for the stitchwork. Make a line of pencil dots 3 in down from the neck curve, all round. The back of the neck is naturally higher than the front, so your points will be higher at the back.

Now join up the dots with a smooth pencil line, and cut. At this stage it is a good idea to work in a few stitches at the ends of the shoulder seams to prevent them running open and driving you to despair before you have even started.

Making the pattern

Faggoting is always done using strong, brown paper. Begin by taking the fabric you have just cut from the neckline, and pinning it onto the paper. Draw around it in pencil, then mark a second outline $\frac{1}{2}$ in wider. This allows you later to join the paper firmly to the blouse:

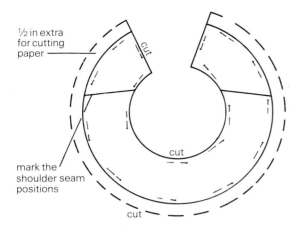

It is helpful to make pencil marks on each side of the shoulder seams, so that you can line them up to give the right neckline shape when you begin faggoting.

Cut out the paper pattern following the outer line. And while the scissors are in your hand, you might as well go on to cut out the rouleaux.

Rouleaux

Take the extra yard of fabric you purchased and, to make sure it is exactly square, fold it diagonally and trim off any surplus.

Tack a row of pins $\frac{1}{2}$ in from the fold and parallel to it. Mark off with a pencil and cut. Opened out, you will have a 1 in wide cross-weave strip, which is used to face the blouse neckline.

Cutting on the cross gives the neckline its curve without wrinkling, and is useful for all kinds of bindings, trimmings and facings.

More cross-cut strips are now needed for the rouleaux. Cut as many as you think you need – each should be $1\frac{1}{2}$ in wide.

If you are planning insertion stitch on the sleeves, too, this is the time to cut some 1 in diagonal strips; enough to face tops of sleeves and armholes in preparation for joining.

Preparing the blouse for faggoting

We are now ready to put the facing on the blouse neckline. Take the first 1 in cross-weave strip and pin it (right sides together) around the raw edge of the scoop.

Tack it into place and machine a seam about $\frac{1}{4}$ in wide. Trim the end and press open.

Make a small hem fold, and pin and tack the facing to the inside of the neckline.

If the first seam gives problems by puckering, open it out again and make a few tiny snips, taking care not to cut too close, catching the seam.

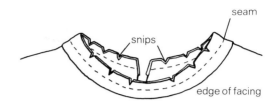

Re-pin the hem in position, and tack and *hem-stitch* the facing to the blouse. Press lightly. The hemstitching, which shows on the right side, can be decorated at intervals with *French knots*.

The next step is to take your brown paper pattern and line it up with the shoulder seams, before pinning it into position behind the scoop you have just completed. Remember, we allowed $\frac{1}{2}$ in on the pattern for this. When you have pinned it all round, tack it firmly into position.

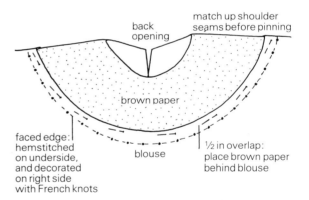

Making the rouleaux

There are two ways of doing this. The method I prefer is to fold the cross-weave strip, right sides facing, and hand sew a small seam about $\frac{1}{4}$ in from the raw edges. I then slip my rouleau needle into the fabric tube. A few firm stitches secure the eye of the needle to the material. Then it is simply a question of ruching-up the material to draw the needle through. As it emerges from the other end it will pull the completed rouleau with it, turning it right side out. Flatten the tube and press lightly along the seam.

Another way is to turn a small hem along each long side of the strip. Bring the two sides together –

the fabric should be right side outwards – and tack along with *running stitch*. When the fabric is later faggoted, the insertion stitch must pass through four layers each time, otherwise tiny gaps will appear when the tacking is removed.

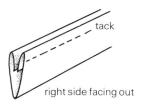

tack

right side facing out

Stitchwork

When you have made up the rouleaux, pin them onto your brown paper pattern, leaving $\frac{1}{4}$ in gaps between each band for the insertion stitch, and secure by tacking.

You will probably find that about four rouleaux are sufficient for a 3 in scoop. Don't forget that the final rouleaux, at the top of the neckline, must be long enough to tie at the back.

The *twisted insertion stitch* can now be worked between the rouleaux (instructions are given on

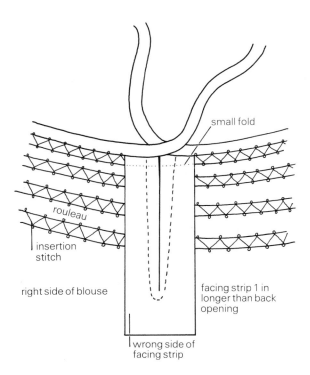

small fold

rouleau

insertion stitch

right side of blouse

facing strip 1 in longer than back opening

wrong side of facing strip

page 114). An additional row joins the faggoting to the blouse.

When you have finished, leave the brown paper in place – the back opening has to be faced next.

On my pattern there was merely a slit, which I faced with a 2 in wide strip of fabric. I made it 1 in longer than the opening, and cut it straight down the centre to within 1 in of the bottom.

Pin the strip over the blouse opening, wrong side uppermost, and tack it into position. It can then be either *backstitched* or machined into place.

Press the facing and snip the edges here and there for a good fit before turning it completely through to the back. Do not forget, at the same time, to snip or tear away the edges of the brown paper.

Now, working inside the back of the blouse, where you have turned the facing through, fold a tiny hem on the outer edge of the strip. Stitch round it to prevent fraying.

From the front, the seam joining the facing to the back can be seen through the faggoting, so fold it inwards once more – completely in half – to hide any raw edges from view:

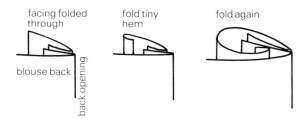

facing folded through

fold tiny hem

fold again

blouse back

back opening

Pin and tack into position behind the faggoting before *hemstitching* around the facing inside the blouse.

The facing can now be pressed, and all the tacking holding the brown paper to the faggoting removed.

The ends of the ties can be turned in and seamed with a few stitches. Decorate the topmost rouleau of the neckline with *French knots* or a few beads.

I find faggoting so enjoyable that I now have the urge to go on and make a blouse with a huge expanse of rouleaux.

Sleeves

If you decide to attempt insertion stitch on the sleeves as well, join the shoulder seams according to your pattern instructions.

Face the armhole and sleeve using the 1 in cross-weave strips you cut earlier:

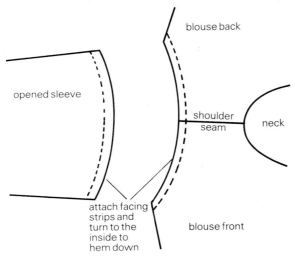

blouse back

opened sleeve

shoulder seam

neck

attach facing strips and turn to the inside to hem down

blouse front

Alternatively, using the seam allowance at the armhole and top of the sleeve, machine a tiny hem, then fold to the reverse and pin down.

When the edges to be joined are finished, remove any tacking and press lightly. Position the open sleeve and armhole $\frac{1}{4}$ in apart, and pin and tack them onto strong brown paper. They can now be joined with *twisted insertion stitch*.

Later, remove the brown paper and make up the side and sleeve seams in the usual way.

The back of the faggoted neckline. I joined the rouleaux to each other and to the blouse with twisted insertion stitch. *The rouleau at the top of the neckline has been left long enough to tie at the back.*

Basic grey-and-white pinstripe blouse with faggoted neckline. The sleeves are joined with insertion stitch.

Table Talk

I spent my childhood fascinated by a huge embroidered table-cloth that my granny made. It was signed by all the members of the family, and brought out for special occasions.

Years later, when I decided to make a table-cloth of my own, I thought it would be nice to continue the tradition. It is embroidered with the signatures of many dear friends and, as many of them have worked with me, it has turned into something of an autograph book.

Granny worked her cloth in patriotic red, white and blue. I chose white silks on white linen, with scalloped edges and a border of drawn threadwork.

On TVS's Afternoon Club I talked briefly about my needlework and mentioned the idea of a cloth of signatures to mark special events such as weddings, christenings or family visits from overseas. The interest from viewers was so enormous that I was asked to embroider a table-cloth step by step each week on the programme.

My Afternoon Club cloth, signed by friends who worked on the show, has alternate *eyelets* and *padded satin dots* set inside the scallops.

The drawn threadwork is 3 in from the scalloping, and worked in *ladder hemstitch*. The signatures are all embroidered in *cord stitch*.

My centre embroidery is in shades of blue and white, and worked on a 10 in frame. Many of the florets are in *long and short stitch*, which is most suitable for blending different grades of coloured silk. Others are in a single shade of *padded satin stitch*.

I made stitch-bars across one of the florets and cut away the inner fabric after edging. The dots and circles are in various stitches: for the tiny ones I used *French knots* or *satin stitch*. Others were made into *eyelets*, bound at the edges, or clusters of *French knots*. The centres of the florets are a selection of all these stitches, to give the hazy blossom effect of a Lace-Cap Hydrangea.

Lace-cap hydrangea.

Opposite *I like to think of these table-cloths as my unusual autograph books. From left to right, they are: the white linen table-cloth signed by friends; my granny's red, white and blue family cloth; and my Afternoon Club cloth, signed by friends who worked on the show.*

Above *Inspired by my granny's embroidered table-cloth, I decided to make one of my own. I have embroidered the signatures of many dear friends in white silks on white linen.*

Collared!

Collars have been the identity mark of period dress down the centuries. Elizabethan, Puritan and Restoration styles are all instantly recognizable by the merest glance at their neckline. And today, thanks to Princess Diana setting the pace, collars (if you will forgive the pun) have come full circle again.

The wonderful things about detachable collars are their long life and versatility. If they are fashioned in classic styles and colours, you can wear them again and again. White collars, even if you like them against dark wools, can simply be unpinned and laundered separately to remain crisp and fresh. Pure silk collars can be nurtured for years without losing their appeal.

Most women like at least one soft white wool sweater in their collection, despite their drawbacks. Not everyone has the complexion to take all that white and, if you wear a coloured shirt underneath, it invariably shows through. Detachable collars solve the problem, and also look good over black, softening the starkness a little.

Surprisingly, they are not difficult to make, so I pass on a few hints and directions for four classic collar styles: a faggoted Peter Pan; a frilled collar with a faggoted edge; an embroidered frilled collar; and a cape collar in broderie anglaise.

It should be enough to get you going. After that, the sky's the limit — there are endless combinations to match anything in your wardrobe. Once you get the hang of the basics, you can design a classic collar for any occasion.

PETER PAN FAGGOTED COLLAR

This is a great favourite of mine. I have used it on clothes I have made because I love its symmetry and simplicity.

There are three ways of cutting a Peter Pan: you can buy a pattern and work from it; pick your size from the neck outlines I have drawn, and follow the steps; or cut a collar by taking a pattern from a sweater or dress. This last method is very useful if the neckline is scooped and you need a precise fit.

What you need
A 27 in square of linen, cotton lawn or silk is enough for a smaller-size collar. Anything larger, or deeper, would take 1 sq yd of fabric to give you room to manoeuvre. If this is your first attempt, try to avoid silk as it is quite slippery to work with You will also need some brown paper and tracing paper.

Using the neck sizes
Select your dress size and trace it from the book.

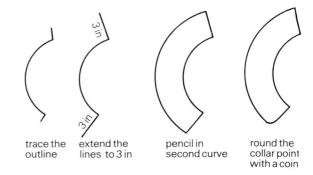

trace the outline

extend the lines to 3 in

pencil in second curve

round the collar point with a coin

To use the pattern, first trace the left-hand half including centre guideline; then move paper across to the right-hand side, line up centre guideline, and trace off the right-hand half.

This, of course, is only half a collar. To complete the pattern, take a piece of brown paper and fold it in half. Lay the 3 in centre-back line of the collar along the fold and draw round the outline. Remember: the neck sizes do not allow for seams, so you must add ¼ in to the size all round:

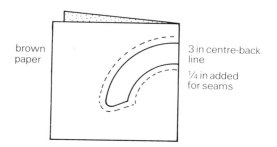

Cut out the collar, open up the brown paper, and you have the full pattern. Now try it out around your neck, or on the sweater or dress you have in mind, and make any adjustments.

You now need to make a second complete paper collar, this time trimming back the front openings and the outer edge by ⅝ in for the rouleau. If you plan to make a double rouleau, take off ¾ in.

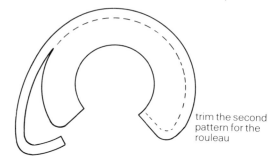

trim the second pattern for the rouleau

Taking a pattern from a sweater or dress
You first have to obtain the exact measurement of the garment by pulling one sleeve inside the other, so that the shoulders lie together and the neck is folded in half.

Pin the shoulder seams together, and put a few more pins around the neck and down the centre-front and back folds.

Now fold a sheet of pattern paper in half and lay it on a flat surface. Pin the back fold of the sweater or dress down the fold of the paper. Support the

fabric with one hand, and smooth out the shape of the neck onto the paper.

When you are sure it looks right, pin around the neck and down the centre-front fold. Follow the outline in pencil.

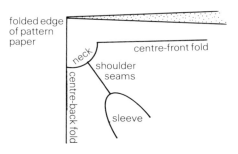

When everything is unpinned, the neck curve and centre-front should be clearly reproduced on your pattern paper. Decide how deep you want your collar to be, remembering that we will be adding on a little for hems and turnings.

In pencil, make the centre-front and centre-back lines 3–4 in long (depending on what you have chosen), and join them with a parallel curve to the neckline:

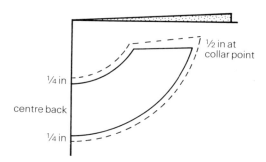

To allow for seams you must now add ¼ in all round. But, to make a perfect fit, the collar point should be extended by ½ in, not a ¼ in. This sounds a little confusing, but it all falls nicely into place later.

Cut out your paper pattern, using a coin to round the collar point. If the centre-back looks rather pointed when you open out the paper, trim it to a gentle curve.

Now pin the pattern to your sweater or dress to make sure it fits, and make any adjustments. You will need a second collar pattern, on strong brown paper, for the faggoting. When you have cut it out, reduce the size of your first collar by ⅝ in to prepare it for the rouleau. Directions are given in the section on faggoting (pages 43–4).

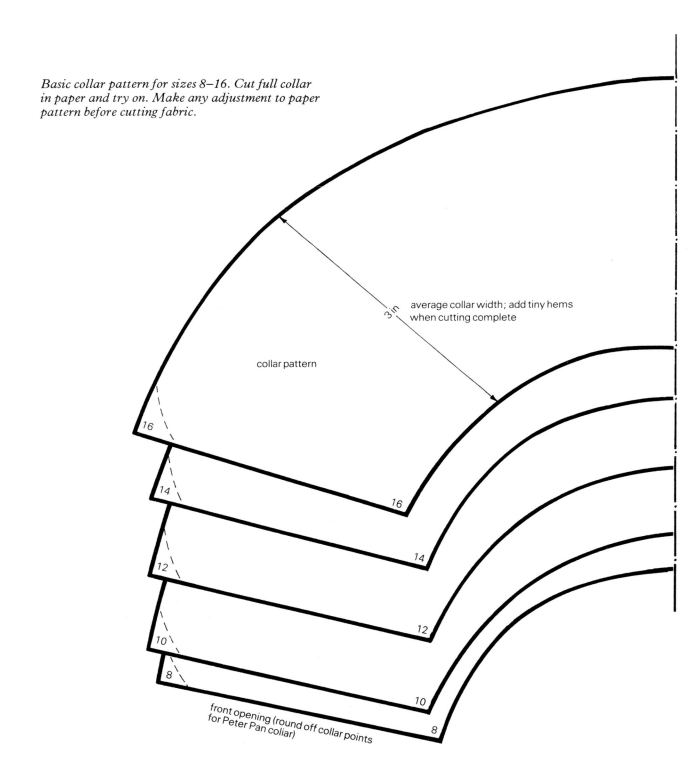

Basic collar pattern for sizes 8–16. Cut full collar in paper and try on. Make any adjustment to paper pattern before cutting fabric.

3 in

average collar width; add tiny hems when cutting complete

collar pattern

16

16

14

14

12

12

10

10

8

8

front opening (round off collar points for Peter Pan coliar)

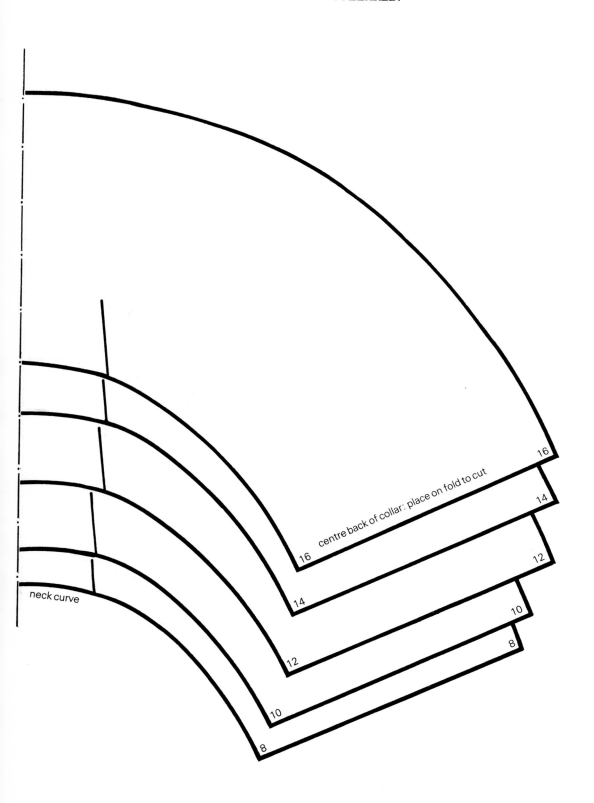

neck curve

centre back of collar: place on fold to cut

16

16

14

14

12

12

10

10

8

8

Cutting out

You now have a large brown paper collar for faggoting, and a smaller pattern (minus the rouleau)
for cutting out the fabric.

Fold your square of fabric in half diagonally,
and place a few pins around it to prevent it slipping.
The collar is cut on the straight grain of the fabric,
through two layers, and the rouleau and neckband
on the cross-weave:

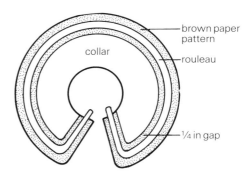

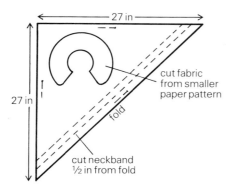

Pin along the diagonal fold and cut the neckband
$\frac{1}{2}$ in from the edge, to give a 1 in wide strip. Now
cut a single rouleau strip, $1\frac{1}{8}$ in wide; for a double
rouleaux cut two strips, each $\frac{3}{4}$ in wide.

Making up the rouleau

Fold the strip in half lengthways and pin and tack.
Backstitch or *running stitch* about $\frac{1}{8}$ in from the
raw edge, right along the strip. Slip your rouleau
needle into the tube and secure the fabric to the
eye with a few stitches. Pull the needle through to
complete the rouleau. Press carefully along the
seam.

Making up the collar

Pin and tack the two collar pieces together (right
sides facing) down the front openings and around
the outside edge, and follow with $\frac{1}{8}$ in seam. When
the stitchwork is complete, turn right side out and
press.

The collar is now ready for faggoting. Pin it
onto the brown paper pattern and, leaving approximately $\frac{1}{4}$ in gap, pin the rouleau around the outside,
making sure that the seam faces the collar.

For a double rouleaux, pin the bands parallel,
leaving even spaces between them.

Tack firmly around both collar and rouleau,
and fill the gap with *twisted insertion stitch*. When
you have finished the faggoting, cut off any excess
rouleau at the neck edge. Snip the tacking and
remove the collar from its brown paper backing.

Attaching the neckband

Pin and tack the collar and neckband together
(right sides facing) by lining up the centre-back of
the collar and the middle of the neckband:

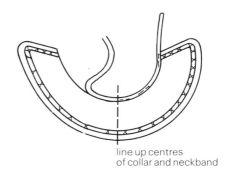

Fastening

You must next decide what type of fastening suits
your collar.

Bow Sew around the neckband in *backstitch*,
then fold it in half and make a small hem on the
inside. *Hemstitch* along both ties, and finish with a
neat turning at the ends.

Fabric button and loop Complete the neckband
as above, but this time make the button side of the
tie 4–5 in long, and the loop side only 2 in. Turn
and stitch the ends.

Pinch the tie on the button side at the neck, and
wind it anti-clockwise around itself into a tight
roll, sewing underneath as you go. Turn the last
$\frac{1}{2}$ in to the back and stitch down. Make a few small
stitches to secure the button to the collar band.

Fold the loop to fit the button and stitch it to
the underside of the collar.

Button fastening Cut off the ties, leaving only
enough for a small turning, and complete the neckband by hemstitching down on the underside. Sew
a small flat button beneath the collar, and make a
buttonhole loop from thread on the other side.

FRILLED AND FAGGOTED COLLAR

This is perhaps the simplest collar to make, as it requires no paper pattern. You could try it on a Liberty print or in simple spots and stripes. It looks particularly good with the insertion stitch worked in a matching colour.

What you need

You will need 1 sq yd of natural fabric, cotton thread in a matching or contrasting colour, and a 4 × 36 in strip of strong brown paper. There will be some fabric left over after cutting the rouleau. You could put it to one side to use for a contrasting rouleau on a self-coloured collar, or for binding or piping for clothes and cushions.

Cutting out

Cut a $3\frac{1}{4}$ in strip straight across the fabric from selvedge to selvedge. Trim the remaining piece to a $32\frac{1}{2}$ in square and fold it diagonally. If you buy 1 metre of material the square will be approximately 36 in, and can be folded without trimming.

Pin the fabric here and there to hold it in place. Measure $\frac{1}{2}$ in from the fold and cut along the diagonal to make the neckband.

Now cut another diagonal strip, $1\frac{1}{4}$ in wide, from a single layer of fabric. Fold it in half lengthways (right sides together) and pin and tack. Make a small seam along it in *backstitch* or *running stitch*, and turn the fabric right side out with your rouleau needle. Press carefully along the seam.

Neckband

The easiest way to achieve a good fit is to hang the neckband strip around your neck, holding the ends to make sure they are the same length. Pinch in the fabric gently at the throat and mark the fastening point with two pins.

The gathered frill will later lie on the central section between the two pins; the fabric at each end will be used to tie your bow.

This is a good time to make up the ties, so fold the neckband in half lengthways, and stitch up to the pins from each end. The ties can then be turned right side out with your rouleau needle!

Faggoting

Take the $3\frac{1}{4}$ × 36 in collar strip, fold the selvedges together and trim them off. Draw a curve on the lower corner and cut through both layers of fabric to round the ends. You can then make a tiny rolled hem along the outer edge:

Press the collar and pin right side uppermost onto your brown paper strip. Leaving a $\frac{1}{4}$ in gap, pin the rouleau parallel to it:

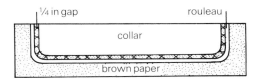

Tack each piece firmly to the brown paper and remove the pins. Work the $\frac{1}{4}$ in space between them with *twisted insertion stitch*. When the embroidery is finished, snip the tacking, remove the brown paper and trim off any excess rouleau.

Joining the collar to the neckband

Work in *running stitch* across the raw edge of the collar and pull it into a gather exactly the width of the pin markers on the neckband. When you have gathered it to the right size, secure the ends of the running stitch and – keeping the gathers as even as you can – pin and tack it onto the neckband (right sides facing).

Backstitch the frill onto the neckband and remove the tacking. To finish off, fold the centre section of the neckband lengthways, and turn a small hem on the wrong side, pinning and tacking as you go. All that is left to be done is to *hemstitch* down – and *voila*!

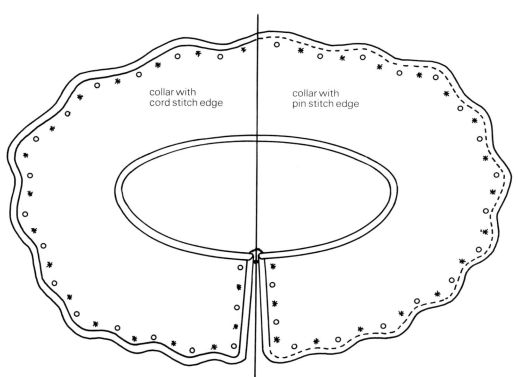

collar with
cord stitch edge

collar with
pin stitch edge

EMBROIDERED FRILLED COLLAR

This is a pretty collar, which can be fastened either front or back, with a single or double frill attached to a neckband.

What you need

The whole collar can be made from about half a yard of fine-weight linen or even-weave cotton. When you buy the fabric, do make sure they cut it completely straight in the shop.

First work out how much you need – measure around the neckline of your dress, sweater or blouse with a strand of wool. Pin it in position as you go, and cut it at the opening of the neckline.

Lay the wool out flat, measure the length, and add $\frac{1}{2}$ in for a small hem at each end.

To make a $16\frac{1}{2}$ in neckband without joins you would need a 13 in square of fabric. A fairly full frill will take twice the length of the material in the neckband. The depth of the frill is, of course, up to you; an average size is approximately $3\frac{1}{2}$ in.

Making up

The frill is cut across the fabric, from selvedge to selvedge. Fold it in half and trim the ends to the size you require, allowing for a $\frac{1}{4}$ in hem at each

end. This is probably the most economical way to cut the fabric:

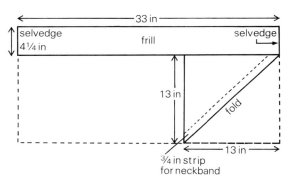

Embroidering the frill

The frill first has to be hemmed on three sides. You can either use *pin stitch*, or hem in *running stitch*, then overcast in a small *satin stitch* to give a fine cord trim.

Opposite *Today, thanks to Princess Diana, collars are popular once more. I've collected them for thirty years, and now have masses of detachable collars in classic styles and colours.*

Pierce a row of evenly-spaced eyelets $\frac{1}{2}$ in up from your pinstitching or cording. They can be interspersed with little *star stitches*, or *double cross stitch*.

When the embroidery is complete, press on the wrong side. Then work small *running stitches* about $\frac{1}{4}$ in from the top, and gather the frill. It should measure about $\frac{1}{2}$ in less than the length of the neckline. Secure the ends of the running stitch with a couple of backward stitches.

Pin the neckband and frill together, right sides facing, along the running stitch – keeping the gathering even as you go. Then tack them together and *backstitch*. Open out and press, then turn in the sides of the neckband by $\frac{1}{4}$ in and press again.

To hem the neckband, fold it in half lengthways and turn a small hem on the underside. Finish each end with invisible stitches.

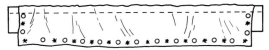

tack frill into place and backstitch

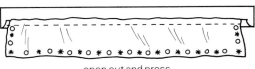

open out and press

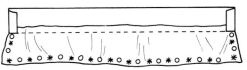

fold in ¼ in at each side

Fastening

Use a buttonhole loop and a tiny flat button, or a hook and eye. If you decide on a hook and eye, *blanket/buttonhole stitch* around the eye in white machine cotton for a neat finish. I prefer buttons on this collar because I find that no matter how careful I am, the hook and eye always manage to peep out.

CAPE COLLAR IN BRODERIE ANGLAISE

The collar requires a yard of 36 in wide linen, and a large sheet of brown paper. If you take your paper pattern to the shop, you may be able to save on fabric by buying from a 48 in length. But remember that the full collar shape has to be cut out twice.

Cutting

The cutting directions are the same as for the Peter Pan collar taken from a sweater or dress (pages 53–6). As the cape collar is larger, you will have to extend the centre-back and front openings to 6 in wide, or even more, before drawing the parallel curve. This collar can, however, be made from a single paper pattern.

When you have cut the pattern, try it on. Bear in mind that it will be $\frac{1}{2}$ in narrower down the front and on the outer curve after scalloping, and you should also allow for a $\frac{1}{4}$ in seam inside the neck curve. Make any small adjustments at this stage before cutting the fabric.

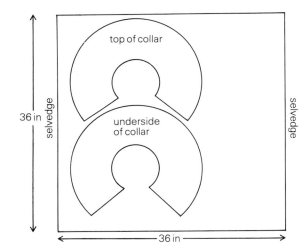

Making up

Pin and tack the two collar pieces, right sides together, and sew a $\frac{1}{4}$ in seam inside the neck curve:

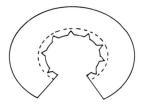

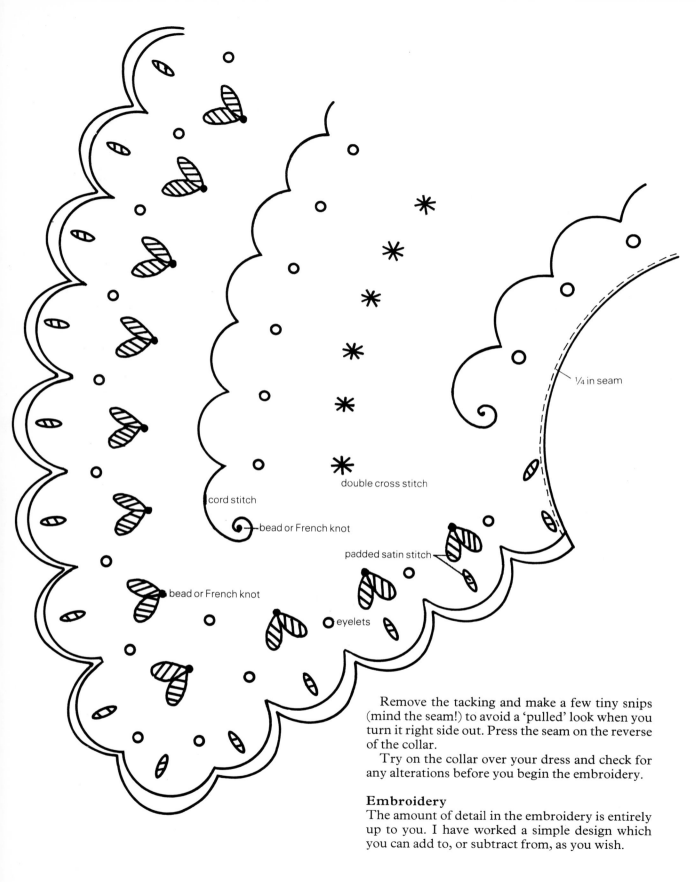

double cross stitch

cord stitch

bead or French knot

padded satin stitch

bead or French knot

eyelets

¼ in seam

Remove the tacking and make a few tiny snips (mind the seam!) to avoid a 'pulled' look when you turn it right side out. Press the seam on the reverse of the collar.

Try on the collar over your dress and check for any alterations before you begin the embroidery.

Embroidery
The amount of detail in the embroidery is entirely up to you. I have worked a simple design which you can add to, or subtract from, as you wish.

It may sound laborious, but I find it better to work out my scallops on the paper pattern first and, when they are right, pencil round them on the fabric. When you are scalloping a curve, it is a good idea also to pencil a line about $\frac{5}{8}$ in inside the outer edge of the fabric, to give yourself a guideline.

Begin the curves at the neck, as the front has to be identical, and use a coin as a template. A 5p

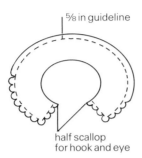

5/8 in guideline

half scallop
for hook and eye

piece is about right, but change to a 10p for the collar points for symmetry.

Trace the embroidery design and transfer it to the fabric using the carbon paper method. Remember to cover it with clean tissue and press with a warm iron to prevent smudging.

A small *running stitch* inside the scalloping outline helps to pad the stitches, and holds the edges together as you sew. Work the scalloping in *buttonhole stitch*, with the loop on the outside edge.

Fastening
Work a buttonhole loop at the neck edge on one side of the collar. Stitch a loop, slightly bigger than a flat shirt button, until it is about three strands thick, and cover in *buttonhole stitch*.

Secure the button on the other side, underneath the collar, keeping the stitches as invisible as possible.

Snippets

Cut work

I don't think I could ever bear to part with my old yellow gingham smock. It was my very first attempt at embroidery, and I made it from an old pair of kitchen curtains.

The smock was started during my first pregnancy, and seemed just the thing. But I spent so much time working on it, that I did not get the opportunity to wear it until I was expecting my second son.

It came into the world as a maternity smock and ended as my sampler – I must have tried every stitch on it. It bears the scars of my earliest efforts at cut work and scalloping, and taught me, too, always to use a frame for embroidery.

Parts of the cut work were quite nerve-wracking. I remember accidentally snipping some of the stitches and having to do them again.

If you would like to try your hand on a smock, or blouse, choose something made from a natural fabric, and preferably one that does not fray easily. Cut work does wonders to a blouse in need of a new look. Pick a garment that washes well and, if it is your first attempt, select a design with only a little cut work involved.

You can use many sewing techniques in cut work and I do not pretend to be an expert. If you stick to the basic rules, however, everything should turn out fine.

When you have transferred the design, outline it in *running stitch* – it helps to hold the shape and gives a little padding to the edge-binding.

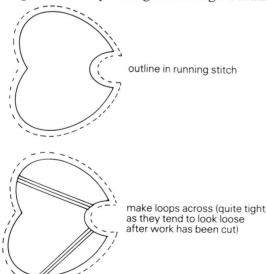

outline in running stitch

make loops across (quite tight as they tend to look loose after work has been cut)

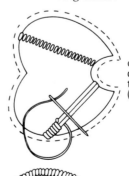

overcast stitch over the bars – do not allow this work to catch the fabric (alternative: buttonhole stitch)

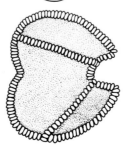

overcast closely all around the outline (alternative stitch: buttonhole stitch – the loops lie on the edge to be cut); cut away the fabric, avoiding the stitch bars and taking care not to catch any of the overcasting; trim again after laundering the complete work

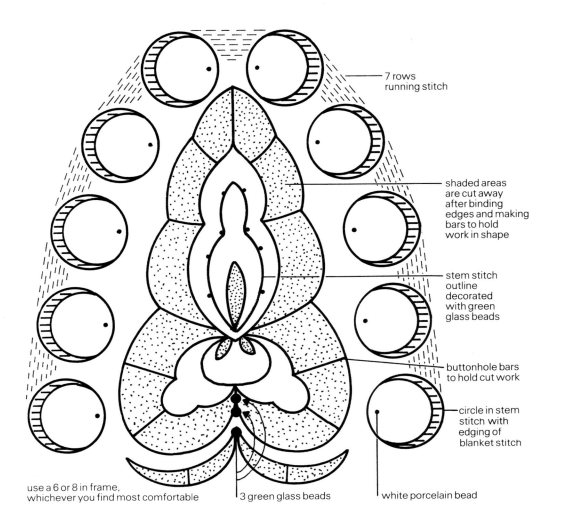

7 rows
running stitch

shaded areas
are cut away
after binding
edges and making
bars to hold
work in shape

stem stitch
outline
decorated
with green
glass beads

buttonhole bars
to hold cut work

circle in stem
stitch with
edging of
blanket stitch

use a 6 or 8 in frame,
whichever you find most comfortable

3 green glass beads

white porcelain bead

*Cut work on yellow gingham smock worked in white
embroidery thread (back).*

Where the cutting is quite extensive, it is best to make stitch-bars across the widest areas for
support. They are worked fairly tightly over the fabric and later overcast, buttonholed over, or
woven. Take care to keep both bars and stitches clear of the fabric to avoid problems when you
cut away.

The outline to be cut should be overcast using even, closely-set *binding* stitches. If you
decide to buttonhole it, the stitch-loops should lie on the edges to be cut.

Snip the fabric carefully away inside the stitchwork and beneath the bars. Any stray threads
can be trimmed after laundering.

WHITE LAWN SMOCK

Lawn is one of my favourite fabrics – it is lovely to wear and launders well.

I incorporated cut work, embroidery and a faggoted collar, which give it a classic, timeless quality. I like it, too, because it is adaptable and versatile – I can wear it demurely buttoned or rakishly open.

The embroidery is in self-coloured silk to fit any colour scheme. You may notice, incidentally, that a few of my embroidery designs are duplicated. Some were first tried out in my early needlework days, but as I go on I expect better standards from myself.

I get enormous pleasure from using a design I like for the second time around, on something different, with the advantage of experience. So, if a motif crops up on a cushion, then again on a shirt, I only hope that when you notice a repeat you also see an improvement!

By the way, the sleeves on this particular smock are possibly the best type for faggoting. The raglan shoulder-to-armhole style cuts across the weave of the fabric and reduces the chance of fraying edges.

(The designs for this smock appear right and on page 68.)

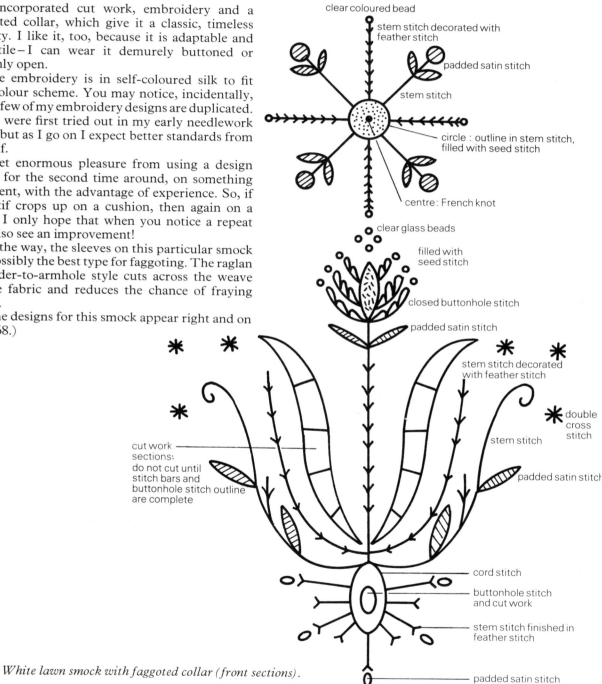

worked in white silk (2 threads as the lawn was so very fine)

clear coloured bead

stem stitch decorated with feather stitch

padded satin stitch

stem stitch

circle : outline in stem stitch, filled with seed stitch

centre: French knot

clear glass beads

filled with seed stitch

closed buttonhole stitch

padded satin stitch

stem stitch decorated with feather stitch

double cross stitch

stem stitch

padded satin stitch

cut work sections: do not cut until stitch bars and buttonhole stitch outline are complete

cord stitch

buttonhole stitch and cut work

stem stitch finished in feather stitch

padded satin stitch

White lawn smock with faggoted collar (front sections).

65

Right *Where the cutting is quite extensive, make stitch-bars across the widest areas for support.*

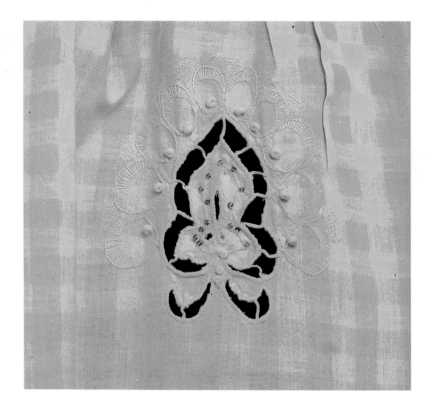

Opposite *The yellow gingham maternity smock is the most special to me, even though it was made from an old pair of kitchen curtains. It was my first attempt at cut work and scalloping.*

Right *Detail of the cut work on the sleeve of the smock. The outline to be cut was overcast using closely-set binding stitches. Of course, I couldn't resist adding a few beads to the finished design.*

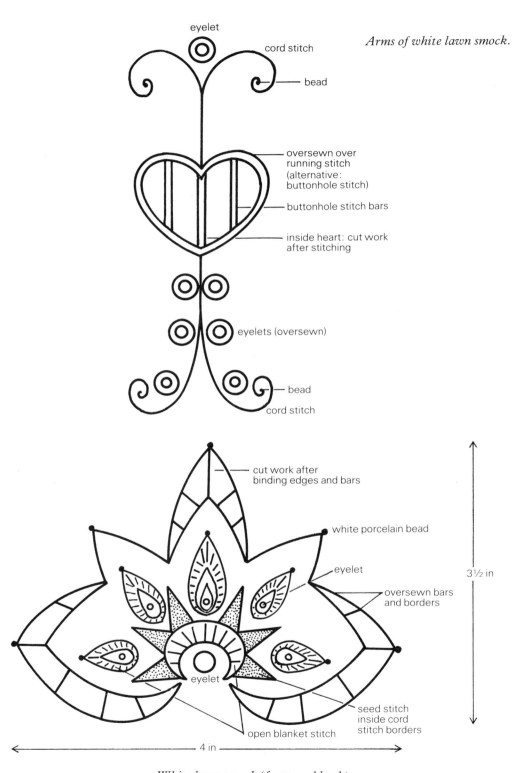

Arms of white lawn smock.

eyelet

cord stitch

bead

oversewn over running stitch (alternative: buttonhole stitch)

buttonhole stitch bars

inside heart: cut work after stitching

eyelets (oversewn)

bead

cord stitch

cut work after binding edges and bars

white porcelain bead

eyelet

oversewn bars and borders

3½ in

eyelet

seed stitch inside cord stitch borders

open blanket stitch

4 in

White lawn smock (front and back).

CREAM LINEN SHIRT

I made this shirt, with a faggoted collar, from medium-weight linen. You might like to use the butterfly design from the back on a shirt or blouse.

The button and buttonhole turnings are decorated with *pin stitching*, which is so simple, but gives a very effective finish.

I completed the whole shirt before attempting the woven bars on the sleeves, which, on reflection, I'm not sure was a good idea. When you draw so many threads on this scale there is a fair amount of 'shrinkage', so it is better suited to fuller sleeves.

Mine turned out a little tight – if you are trying this type of work, add extra width for the embroidery before making up the sleeves. Any size adjustments can be made before you set them in the shirt. A word of caution, though: woven bars take an incredibly long time to do.

Back – vertical embroidery rows
The vertical lines of embroidery from neckline to hem are worked along the fabric grain in three rows of *four-sided stitch* on each side of the butterfly. The shorter lines are three rows of *coil filling stitch*, each ending in an eyelet hole.

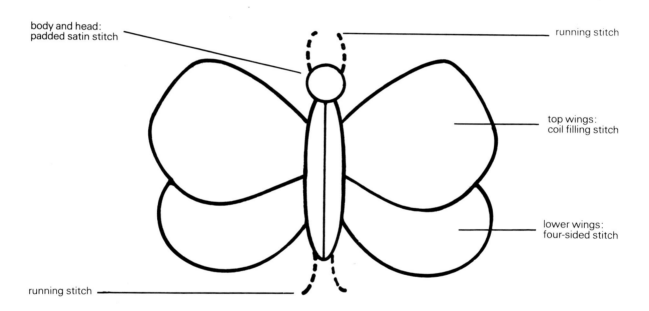

body and head:
padded satin stitch

running stitch

top wings:
coil filling stitch

lower wings:
four-sided stitch

running stitch

Back centre embroidery.

Above *Embroidery design at the front hem of the white lawn smock. I used self-coloured silk for the embroidery work, to fit any colour scheme.*

Above left *Embroidery design on the back of the white lawn smock. I often duplicate embroidery designs, hopefully improving their standard each ,time.*

Left *Butterfly embroidery design on the back of the cream linen shirt.*

Opposite *The Una Stubbs collection.*

butterflies, all white:
body – padded satin stitch;
wings – running stitch and seeding stitch

flowers:
white, in long
and short stitch,
with blue French
knots in centre

buds:
blue and white,
in long and short stitch

Sheet turn-back.

roses:
shaded
in pink and white,
long and short stitch

leaves:
silver green,
mostly worked
in feather stitch
and stem stitch

Good Night Ladies . . .

There is nothing quite like the sensuous luxury of freshly-laundered bed linen. Synthetic materials never quite capture the unique country-air smell of natural fabric. And when it is enhanced with pretty embroidery I find it, well, little short of paradise.

Most of my sheets and pillow-cases are monogrammed. The lettering styles vary slightly, but they are mainly worked in *padded satin stitch*, with a little embellishment.

I have used designs, such as roses and barley, on sets of bed linen, and next I plan to work some lettered borders along the turn-back of my sheets. They might make an unusual gift: 'Good Night, Sleep Tight' for a child's bed; 'Do Not Disturb' as a wedding present; even 'Caution – Man Working Overhead' if you wish to be naughty. Or how about simply 'Men At Work' for gay friends?

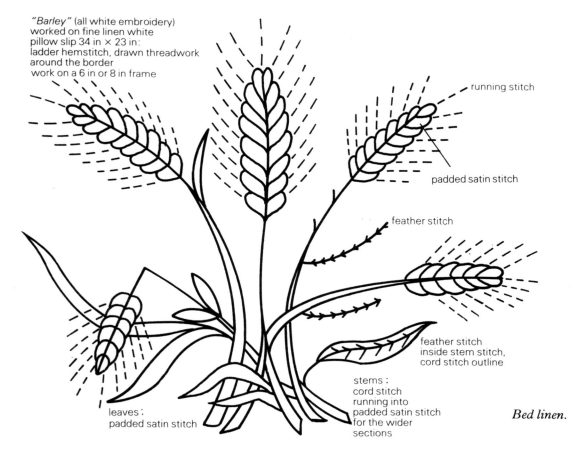

"Barley" (all white embroidery)
worked on fine linen white
pillow slip 34 in × 23 in:
ladder hemstitch, drawn threadwork
around the border
work on a 6 in or 8 in frame

running stitch

padded satin stitch

feather stitch

feather stitch
inside stem stitch,
cord stitch outline

leaves :
padded satin stitch

stems :
cord stitch
running into
padded satin stitch
for the wider
sections

Bed linen.

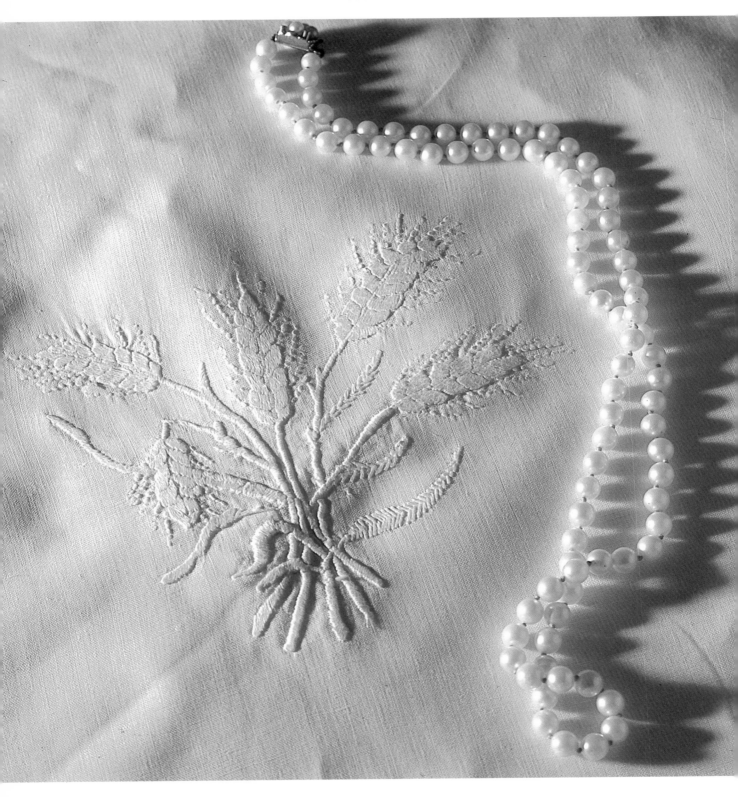

Above *Like most of my bed linen, this pillow-case has been monogrammed. Although I tend to vary lettering styles slightly from item to item, the monograms are mainly worked in* padded satin stitch, *with a little embellishment.*

Opposite *This barley design forms the centre-piece for a set of pillows.*

If you buy iron-on transfers for monogramming, they are always printed in a mirror-image. When you design your own, use the old-fashioned carbon paper method to transfer them to your fabric.

Do remember: if you need to secure the design with pins, be sure not to pin through the carbon. It will leave marks on your sheet, which can be confusing. 'Fix' the finished design to the linen by covering with clean tissue and pressing with a warm iron.

If the designs from my bed linen catch your eye, copy them onto your sheet-corners or pillow-cases using the same technique. The needlework on the roses is uncomplicated – mostly *long and short stitch*. The barley was embroidered as a centre-piece for a set of pillows.

I was pleased with the result because it looks so pretty in my bedroom. The only problem, of course, is that you lose all inclination to get up.

A HERB PILLOW

I made this small pillow on holiday in Greece in 1979. It does not, of course, have to be filled with herbs. You can use it as a baby's cradle pillow, for travelling, or simply lounging – though this does also require a long cigarette holder and heavy eyelids.

My pillow is about 12 in sq but, if you wish to work from a small pillow you may already have, measure it up and add 2 in to the overall dimensions for scalloping.

What you need
The whole pillow can be made from just 12 in of 36 in wide white linen. You will also need two small flat buttons and some white embroidery silk. I added a few white porcelain beads, but if yours is intended for a baby, then it would be better to leave them out.

Incidentally, if you do decide to use beads, try to avoid the pearlized type. They are fine for knitwear, but do not retain their finish in high-temperature washes.

How to make it
The pillow is made from two pieces of fine linen: a 15 × 12 in rectangle for the back, and a 12 in square for the front:

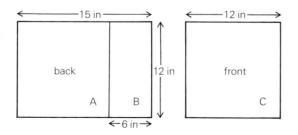

I began by taking the longer, back cover and cutting a 6 in vertical strip from the end (section B in the diagram). I then folded and turned a $\frac{1}{2}$ in hem along the scissor line of A and B:

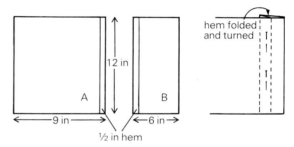

Sew and press the hem – it is always easier to press as you go along.

Now lay the hem of piece B over the hem of piece A, and pin and tack them together. They now make a 12 in square.

Turn the fabric over to the back and stitch the hemmed sections together with a 2 in seam at the top and bottom. The 8 in opening will be used to stuff the pillow through, and will be buttoned.

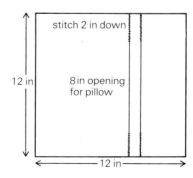

Press again and flatten the seams. The back is now ready for buttons and button-loops.

Sew the buttons onto piece A, and then make

two tiny pencil dots on either side of each button on the hem of piece B.

Each loop is made from about half a dozen single-strand loops of silk. Be sure to catch the fabric each time with a tiny stitch. Cover all six loops in *buttonhole stitch*:

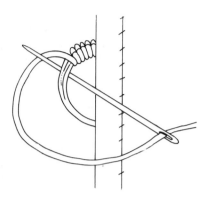

Finally, as a guide for joining the cushion together, centre a 10 in pencil square on both back and front covers. All the groundwork is now complete.

Embroidery

An 8 in frame is suitable for the stitchwork. The design (on page 80) should be centred on the front cover using carbon paper; then embroider following the stitch guide. Press on the wrong side when you have finished.

I made two squares of drawn threadwork to frame the freestyle embroidery by drawing a 9 in square, and an 8¼ in square inside it.

The smaller square is worked in *ladder hemstitch*,

in the same style as used in the first of the cushion projects (page 32). The 9 in square is a few threads wider, and is also done in *ladder hemstitch*. As a contrast, join the bars in groups of three with a central thread of machine cotton to give a star effect.

After pressing, the front and back can be pinned together along the sides of the 10 in square. Secure them with *running stitch* and cover in *cord stitch*.

I drew the pillow-case scallops with a coin on a 12 in sq paper pattern. When you are happy with the outline, pin it to the front cover and draw around the curves in pencil.

Mark an inner stitchline before sewing, and do not cut away the fabric until the buttonholing is finished:

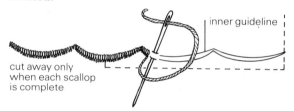

The eyelet positions are marked in pencil and worked in running stitch, before piercing with a stiletto. Fold back the ragged edges and oversew evenly.

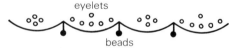

The scallops can be finished with beads, attached with tiny hidden stitches in strong white thread. Before you show your pillow off, remember to sign and date it.

Opposite *Embroidered bed linen. In the past I have tended to use traditional designs, such as the roses on the turn-back of the sheet.*

Above *Fine-linen herb pillow, with flower embroidery design.*

Herb pillow embroidery.

 Inner flower head: *padded satin stitch.*

Stamen: *cord stitch* – the outline is covered in *running stitch* and overlaid with a close *satin stitch* to give a cord effect. Finish with knots or beads.

Outer flower head: *cord stitch*, sometimes called *overcast stitch.*

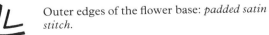 Leaves: two *bullion knots* laid side by side to give a leaf effect.

Stems: *cord stitch* or *stem stitch.*

Outer edges of the flower base: *padded satin stitch.*

Inner leaves of the flower base: *padded satin stitch.*

 Filling stitch: a *small running stitch.*

Embroidery on Knitwear

A classic touch of embroidery can give a new lease of life to a plain wool or cashmere sweater. With a little imagination you can make a chain-store woolly look like designer knitwear – and a Sloane Ranger on a galloping horse couldn't detect the difference.

Embroidering onto knitwear is not difficult, but it has to be worked from the wrong side with a mirror image of your design.

If you have a favourite flower, or animal, you would like to embroider on your sweater, draw it on paper first. Then make a 'sandwich' by placing a sheet of carbon paper face up on the table. On top of this goes a piece of muslin, big enough to take the motif, followed by the design itself. When you re-trace the outline, the mirror image will be carried onto the muslin.

Cut the muslin to a workable size and pin and tack it with small stitches to the reverse of your sweater. You can check that you have it in the right place from the tacking lines on the right side.

The muslin prevents the wool from stretching and distorting your design as you embroider.

Use *satin stitch* as it has the same appearance on each side – but do keep an eye on the progress of the stitching on the right side as you go.

When you have finished, the muslin should be trimmed back as far as possible. The front of the embroidery can then be given any final touches, such as knots or beads.

You could, of course, monogram your sweater, or even add a brand-name. Instead of Lacoste or Dior on a really nice cashmere sweater, why not Tesco or Woolworth? It would certainly turn a few heads. Unpick the Saab or Porsche from your man's sweater and substitute Reliant Robin or Cortina.

I have seen people with Bowie discreetly embroidered on their knitwear. Bowie, like Gucci, doesn't need the publicity. A neat little Frank Ifield or Ruby Murray would be much more appropriate.

What a Card!

Embroidered greeting cards are personal and quite unique. Nothing off the shelf, however sumptuous or expensive, can hope to match them.

A tiny needlework card can be stitched in an evening or two from scraps of silk or linen. If it's a Valentine it will get the message across far more effectively than any four-foot padded heart in throbbing nylon.

I always make small, simple cards because much of my embroidery tends to be minute. Given a little patience, they are easy – and inexpensive – to do. A man's linen handkerchief, perhaps one of those unused gifts still around from last Christmas, is enough to produce half a dozen for various occasions.

Keep them simple and personal: for a fanatical jogger you could, for instance, embroider a single sneaker disappearing out of the corner of the card. A hamburger and a bottle of ketchup might suit a teenager who loves junk food.

How to mount them

You need to invest in some card, a tube of glue, and a Stanley knife. You probably already have a scrap of fine linen and enough snippets of thread in your work-box. My cards measure $3\frac{1}{2} \times 4$ in with a $2\frac{1}{2} \times 3$ in embroidered linen inset.

The card itself, perhaps white or buff coloured, is 7×4 in and folded by scoring down the centre with scissors. On the front, centre a $2\frac{1}{2} \times 3$ in panel in pencil and cut it out carefully with a Stanley knife. Use a new blade if possible, and press hard in the corners to get a clean edge.

Ovals and circles require a very steady hand and a good template. They can look home-made if you are not careful.

When you have cut out the centre panel, you may want to outline the edges with a silver or gold pen, or any other colour that matches the embroidery.

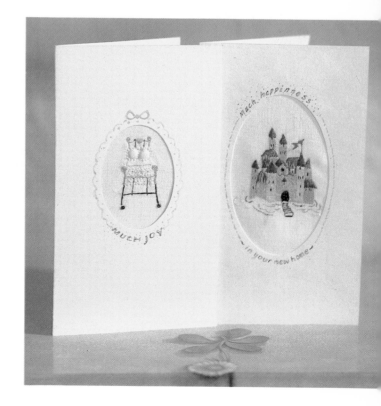

Right   Use materials imaginatively when embroidering cards. For example, I used brass-coloured embroidery silk with touches of gold foil thread for the bedstead, and black beads for the castors of the bed on the wedding congratulations card. For the change of address card, I used several grades of peachy pink thread to make the brickwork look realistic.

You can vary the size and shape of the card according to the style of the embroidery. The linen should be about $\frac{1}{2}$ in wider than the window. Dab a little glue around the edges of the linen and inside the back of the cut-out frame, and bring them gently together. Do make sure the glue is dry before you try. I remember abandoning my first attempt because I squeezed too hard and ruined the embroidery.

The back of the linen is covered with a piece of thin card fractionally smaller than the front panel:

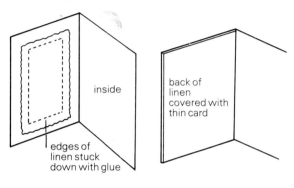

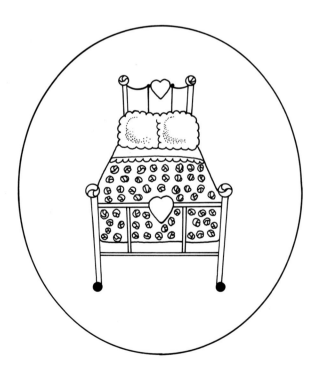

Wedding congratulations.

WEDDING CONGRATULATIONS

This could have all the makings of a miniature masterpiece. Originally I worked the bedstead solely in flat gold thread, but I thought it looked a little too brassy.

I am much happier with the Una Mark II model: brass-coloured embroidery silk with touches of gold foil thread here and there. The little knobs and castors can be black beads or *French knots*.

The hearts at the head and foot of the bed are worked in a blend of turquoise, pink and white to give a mother-of-pearl effect, but you could fill them with a tiny cluster of mother-of-pearl beads if you wish.

I decided to do the bedspread in *four-sided stitch* with *French knots*. On the other hand, if you prefer a wooden bed, you could try a patchwork quilt. The outline of the patches would first have to be drawn in pencil, and filled with threads of different colours.

The edge of the turn-back on the sheets is scalloped below a tiny line of drawn threadwork.

I did the pillows in *long and short stitch*, with a *satin stitch* frill, and plumped them up with padding. All you have to do is to tack a strip of fine butter muslin on the back of the fabric and stitch a little window around each pillow. Remove the tacking and make a small opening in the muslin behind each pillow. With the point of a stiletto, or a pair of tweezers, gently stuff in some cotton wool. When you have stitched up the openings, the pillow will look quite fat and dumpy. This is known as trapunto, or stuffed quilting.

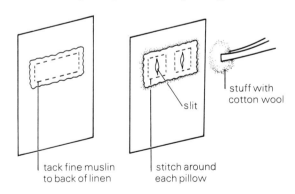

A BIRTH OR CHRISTENING

The nappy pin is embroidered to look as if it has been stuck through the linen. To add a touch of realism you could even use a piece of Terry towelling.

I used flat silver thread that looks like foil, and silver-grey reel cotton. If you know the sex of the baby, you could make the pin in blue or pink instead.

The two threads should each be brought up to the right side of the linen at the same point. Lay the silver thread along the line of the design, holding it with your thumb as you go. Tie it down at regular intervals with tiny *couching stitches* in silver-grey. Remember to keep your threads long enough to go through the back to finish off.

PASSING A DRIVING TEST

Passing your test is such a milestone that it deserves a special card. I embroidered mine on fine white linen, edged the discarded L-plates in pale grey *stem stitch*, and filled the squares with *long and short stitch* in white.

The Ls themselves are done in bright red embroidery silk, worked in *satin stitch*.

I thought the cloud of exhaust smoke looked best in shades of pale and dark grey embroidery silk, but it can be just as effective in reel thread. I worked mine in *cord stitch*.

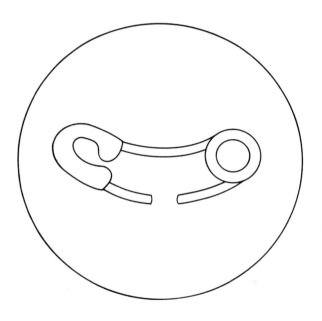

A birth or christening.

Passing a driving test.

CHANGE OF ADDRESS

Friends moving house will give this pride of place – a small, turretted castle topped with a brave little flag, and a tiny 'sold' sign in the corner. It would be nice to embroider their initials on the flag, or even a few flying bats emerging from the roof.

The roofs are in slate grey *straight stitch* and the windows and turrets are worked in a darker *straight stitch*. All the brickwork is in several grades of peachy pink *long and short stitch*. The rounded parts are emphasized with paler shades where they protrude. It is helpful to draw shading lines as a guide for rounding the stitches.

The drawbridge is simply outlined, and the rope and steps are in *straight stitch*.

As the outlines are all so delicate, I bought some fine silk threads from the Royal School of Needlework and worked them in *split stitch*.

FORGET-ME-NOT

If someone owes you a letter, or the love of your life is away for a while, why not make him or her a card as a pretty reminder. If that fails, they would be advised not to come home!

Use a photograph of yourself looking glum surrounded with forget-me-nots, or perhaps a simple caricature of your face. Emphasize your eyes, hair or cheeks to make it instantly recognizable, and add a single, clear glass bead for a tear.

Forget-me-not.

Change of address.

Opposite *No shop-bought card can hope to match one you have embroidered especially for the occasion, whatever it may be.*

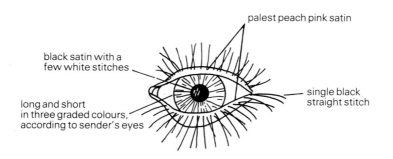

black satin with a
few white stitches

palest peach pink satin

single black
straight stitch

long and short
in three graded colours,
according to sender's eyes

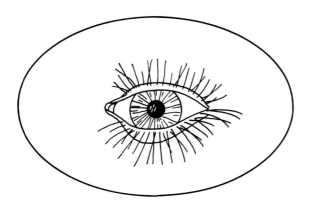

'I've got my eye on you'.

'I'VE GOT MY EYE ON YOU'

This can be used at any time of the year.

For the outline, try *satin stitch* in the palest peachy pink. Embroider the iris in *long and short stitch* in your own eye colour, using three graded shades for a natural effect. The lashes are black *single straight stitch*, minus mascara of course! Work the pupil in black *satin stitch* with a few white highlights.

If you wanted the message to be more obvious, you could embroider the pupil as a tiny padded heart.

VALENTINES

If you prefer a traditional valentine, you might like to try some little fat padded hearts in scarlet on white linen. Use *padded satin stitch*, and add just a few *French knots* and bright red glass beads.

For the large heart I worked *long and short stitch*; then, turning to the back, I covered it with butter muslin and stitched around the shape. Take care to keep the stitches invisible on the right side. To pad it, cut a tiny window in the muslin, poke a little cotton wool inside and stitch the muslin together again.

Valentines.

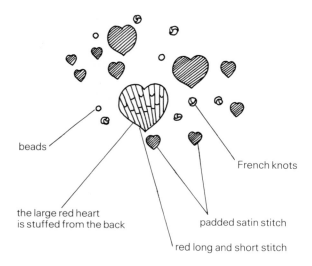

beads

the large red heart
is stuffed from the back

French knots

padded satin stitch

red long and short stitch

89

Family Album

Photograph albums are special. Families and friends pore lovingly over them, so why not give yours an eye-catching cover?

My own has a picture of our home embroidered on the front, with family signatures on the back. If you find that your snaps tend to spill over into boxes and envelopes, you could give them a new home by making covered albums for special occasions such as weddings, birthdays and family gatherings.

Guests could be invited to sign the cover, and later you could embroider their names.

An embroidered picture of your family standing in front of your house would be nice. A holiday album cover could be designed from a photograph of a place that you have stayed in to give a record of, say, the Kenyan holiday, or the Greek holiday.

Or divide it into sections and get your children to make a drawing for each – they can easily be copied onto fabric using carbon paper.

Making the cover
I chose a 36 in wide, heavy-grade linen to cover the front, spine and back of the album with turn-ins for the sleeves.

Measure the depth of your album and add about 2 in for a small hem at the top and bottom.

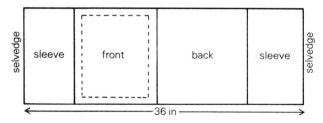

Pin the fabric around the album, wrong side outwards, and mark with pins or a pencil the area on the front cover to be embroidered. You should also mark with a pin the exact depth of the hem along the top and bottom. Incidentally, if you make use of the selvedges you will not need to hem the inner edge of the sleeves that hold the album inside the cover.

Embroidery
Draw your design on paper and transfer it to fabric using carbon paper. Use an embroidery frame if you have one large enough – if not, an old picture frame and drawing pins will do. Large pieces of embroidery can look 'pulled' if you do not take care to maintain an even tension.

If the thought of choosing colours and stitches as you work paralyses you with indecision, colour your paper design with crayons before you begin.

Match the colours with silks already in your workbox and, if you need more, make up a small chart to take with you when you go shopping.

Your sampler, if you have one, will help you decide which are the best stitches to use. As most of them fall into family groups, this is where a good stitch book comes in useful.

For outlines, choose stitches such as *cord, stem, split, running stitch, backstitch,* and so on. Filling stitches, such as *long and short stitch* and *satin*

Opposite The family photograph album, with a picture of our home embroidered on the front.

stitch, are effective for shading. Rounded and angular shapes can be created by choosing shades of the same colour.

When you require perspective lines, mark them on your fabric as a guide. If you are filling in areas, stitch at different angles, working in sections within the guidelines.

For instance, on a leaf, angle the stitches on each side of the centre vein, and use silks two grades darker for the underside where the leaf curls. Set the stitches at different angles to those on the top side of the leaf.

Try to vary textures by using different filling stitches wherever you can. *Seeding*, *couching*, *sheaf stitch* and *chain stitch* are particularly useful. A thoughtful sprinkling of *knots* and *lazy daisy stitch* can suggest the hazy blossoms of impressionist paintings.

This is an ideal opportunity to experiment with new stitches. Take your time planning the stitches, and with the help of a good stitch book, try them on your sampler first. I love preparing work, and often take days planning the smallest piece. Do try, above anything, to aim for creative and artistic satisfaction in your stitchwork. I am always striving to improve my work technically, but never at the price of stifling inspiration.

Finishing

When you have completed your embroidery, remove the tacking outline and lay your work face down on a soft pad. Cover with a damp cloth and press.

Pin and tack the hems along the top and bottom with a single fold. Hem in *herringbone stitch*, which both covers the raw edge and holds down the turnover without creating a bumpy effect. The stitch should be worked from left to right:

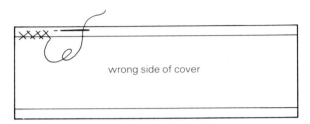

wrong side of cover

Remove the tacking and wrap the cover around the album, folding in the sleeves for a snug fit. Mark the line of the folds with pins, making sure that they lie straight.

Take out the album and fold the sleeves into place with the pins as a guide. Pin and tack along the top and bottom of each turning and oversew neatly. Take care to make a strong finish at each edge where the album will be slipped in and out.

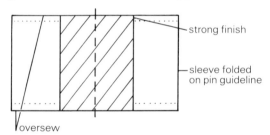

strong finish

sleeve folded on pin guideline

oversew

Remove any pins and tacking. Turn right side out, and slip in the album to decide if your work needs a final pressing.

A Granny Cami

By the time I felt ready to tackle a camisole, my needlework was much improved. Camisoles are, in fact, really quite simple to make – as long as you take your time and keep a cool head!

All the patience and dedication that women put into stitchwork years ago is worth recreating, especially on something you can wear so often. The cami I had in mind looks pretty under an open shirt, a suit, organdie blouse, or simply on its own.

Above all, I wanted it to look original; if possible, indistinguishable from something granny might have made. It sounds a tall order, but not as difficult as you might think.

For the fabric, I used the best of an old linen sheet passed on by my mother-in-law. I bought a pattern and adapted it very simply for the pin-tucking and embroidery. Later, I worked out an easy measure-yourself method which is worth trying.

What you need
If you do not fancy cannibalizing the family sheets, buy 1¼ yd of fine linen, approximately 35 in wide. If it is not pre-shrunk, add a few inches all round. In either case, wash and press the fabric before cutting out.

You will also need: 1 yd of ¾ in white cotton tape; about ¾ yd of narrow knicker elastic; a reel of strong white cotton; and half a dozen pearl shirt buttons.

Good linen is expensive, but lovely to work with – and it lasts a lifetime. All the stitchwork that goes into making it beautiful takes time, so it is important to make absolutely sure the cami is a good fit before embarking on it.

I once spent a whole year, on and off, making an intricate blouse. When I tried it on, the sleeves were too tight – so now I'm searching for someone with sparrow's arms.

The best way is to cut it out in pattern paper first – a cheap remnant of fabric will do equally well – then tack it together and try it on. Besides, think of all the smashed crockery you'll save by getting it right!

Measuring up
The first step is to measure your bust, divide by two, then add on about 2 in for hems and shaping (e.g., 34 in bust divided by 2 = 17 in; add 2 in = 19 in).

Now measure yourself underarm to hip, adding 2 in to allow for a blouson effect.

Back pattern
To start your pattern for the back of the cami, cut a squarish piece of paper, using your bust measurement for the width, and the armpit-to-hip figure for the depth.

Now fold it across from left to right. If you are a 34 in bust it should look something like this:

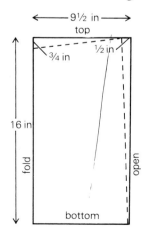

Opposite *An embroidered, pin tucked camisole, which I made from an old linen sheet.*

Above *The camisole is embroidered both on the front and the back. When embroidering the front panels, do remember that the design should be at least 6 in from the bottom of the cami to allow for the elastic gathering.*

Notice the dotted lines. I measured $\frac{3}{4}$ in down in the top left corner, and took the line in a gentle curve to the top right to make the outline of the centre-back.

Another line runs from a point $\frac{1}{2}$ in from the top right-hand corner, straight down to the bottom right corner. This is to shape the underarm. Now cut the paper along the dotted lines.

Incidentally, if you are as forgetful as I am, it's a good idea at this stage to mark the pattern TOP and BOTTOM.

Front pattern

This time, instead of folding the paper, make the pattern in two separate halves. But first add $2\frac{1}{2}$ in to the size of the outline. The extra width allows for pin-tucks and helps give the cami a loose effect. The extra length allows for adjustment on the bust and armhole-shaping at the sides.

So, again working to that 34 in bust, each front half should look like this:

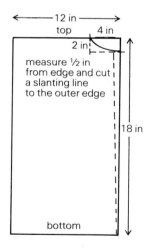

To draw in the underarm curves, square off a section in the top right-hand corner about 2 in deep and 4 in wide (the dotted lines in the diagram). This is just a handy guide for shaping the underarm. Now draw in the curve; if doing it freehand gives you the jitters, a plate or saucer might help.

By this stage you may detect a pleasant glow of efficient satisfaction. Capitalize on it immediately by thinking ahead to the facing for the buttons and buttonholes.

Two strips, the same depth as the front pattern and 2 in wide, will do nicely:

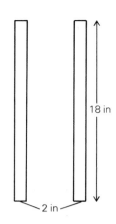

Assembly

By now you should have five pattern pieces. (Together they will take up about half the fabric, leaving plenty over for shoulder straps and front and back facings.)

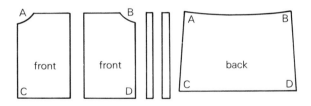

Now lift the two fronts and place them on the back pattern. Before pinning lines AC together, make sure that corner A of the back meets the bottom of the armhole curve of front corner A.

Repeat by joining the other front piece to the back along line BD. I allowed myself about $\frac{1}{2}$ in for fine seams.

Next, take the button and buttonhole strips and fold them lengthways to make a guideline for finishing later. Pin one down each edge of the centre-front openings.

The pattern is almost ready to try on. Just one final piece of forward-planning: draw a line, about $\frac{1}{2}$ in from the edge, down each front opening. From this line, fold and pin a 2 in wide tuck down each front half, top to bottom. This is equal to the material that will be taken up by decorative pin-tucks, and ensures you a good fit.

With the button strips in position, and the 2 in tuck in place, it should look something like this:

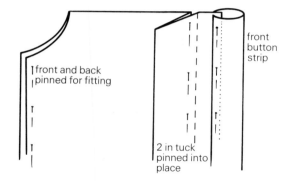

Try it on gingerly. Pins can be pretty lethal weapons, so make sure they point downwards, away from the underarms.

Check the armhole curves carefully. Now is the time to make adjustments and corrections – remember that crockery bill! The whole thing should be slightly long and loose – later the elastic will draw it in and up to give a blouson effect.

Phew! Treat yourself to a cuppa – the rest, by comparison, is far less nerve-wracking.

Facings

Now you can unpin the paper pattern pieces and make the facing patterns: two for the front and one for the back. They are identical to the original front and back patterns in width, but only a few inches deep.

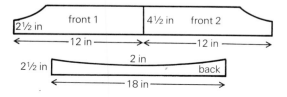

When they are complete, smooth out your linen and lay out all your pattern pieces on it as shown on page 98.

Straps

This is a good time to make the cami's shoestring shoulder straps. First fold the 16 in square of linen diagonally. Then pin a line 3 in from the fold and parallel to it, followed by another line of pins just ½ in from the fold (see page 98).

Between the two rows of pins, draw a line across the fabric, just over 1 in from the crease, and cut. Now, leaving all the pins in position, cut along the fold itself, taking care not to pull the fabric. This

leaves you with two cross-weave strips, each a little over 1 in wide. Remove the pins holding the two pieces together, and trim the ends square.

It is a good idea to seam the straps at this point, so that they are ready for joining to the cami when the time comes.

Fold each strip in half lengthways, pin, and then *backstitch* a very narrow seam.

Take a rouleau needle and slide it into the completed band. Rouleaux are hard to come by in most shops, so you could instead settle for a knitter's needle – the type with a large eye and blunt end. However, they do not have the advantage of the rouleau's length, which makes the job so much easier.

So, with the needle inside the band, stitch the eye firmly to the end of the fabric. Then simply ruche-up the band and pull the needle through.

Snip off the cotton joining linen and rouleau needle, and press the fabric carefully. The two shoestring straps can now be put to one side. Onward, ladies!

The back

Lay your back on a flat surface (no madam, the back of the *cami* – this is no time for a rest). At the bottom, mark a point, in pencil, 4 in in from the right-hand corner, and draw out a vertical thread. Repeat on the other side.

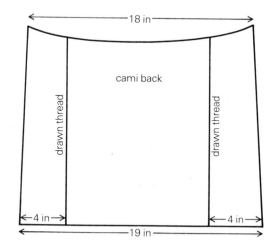

Embroidering the back

For the freestyle embroidery you will need to use an 8 in frame for the main panel. Transfer the pattern, using carbon paper, onto the centre-back. The top corners of the design should be approximately ¾ in from the top of the cami back, and can be done with a tiny frame.

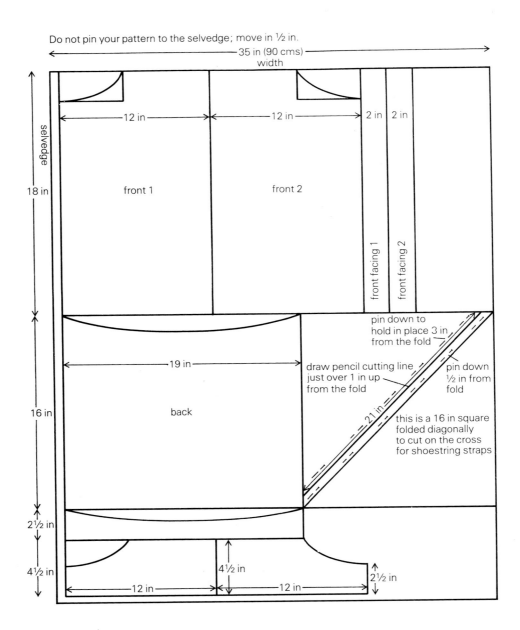

Do not pin your pattern to the selvedge; move in ½ in.

35 in (90 cms) width

selvedge

18 in

12 in
12 in
2 in
2 in

front 1
front 2

front facing 1
front facing 2

16 in

19 in

back

pin down to
hold in place 3 in
from the fold

draw pencil cutting line
just over 1 in up
from the fold

pin down
½ in from
fold

21 in

this is a 16 in square
folded diagonally
to cut on the cross
for shoestring straps

2½ in

4½ in

4½ in

2½ in

12 in
12 in

Arrangement of paper pattern pieces on piece of fabric.

The back of the camisole showing the embroidered design and drawn threadwork.

Cami—back embroidery.

A glossary of the stitches used can be found at the back of the book (pages 107–14).

Drawn threadwork

There are two rows of drawn threadwork, and about five or six threads are drawn for each. If your fabric is fine, you may wish to draw out a few more to make a wider panel. As the threads will be pulled completely out, it is not necessary to darn the edges.

It is easier if you turn the piece sideways and work from right to left in *ladder hemstitch*. Do take care to keep an even tension on the stitchwork, so that you don't 'shrink' the fabric as you go.

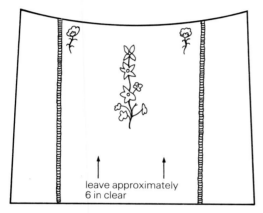

leave approximately 6 in clear

The back is now complete and, with a little luck, should be the same size as its paper pattern. Remember to press it on the wrong side before you put it aside.

Cami front

Take the two front pieces and press a small hem along the top of each. Make sure it stays in place as you next pin and tack on the button and button-

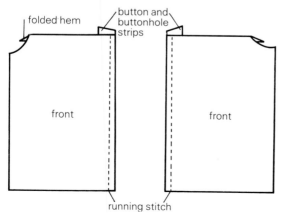

folded hem

button and buttonhole strips

front   front

running stitch

hole strips. They will obviously be a little longer at the top because of the hem you have just made, so don't panic. I used a small *running stitch* to set them in, but you can machine it if you prefer.

Now open and press the button facing seams, make a neat hem along the top and tack with coloured thread.

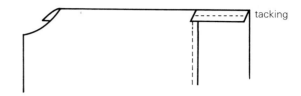

tacking

The whole of the facing can now be folded round, over the front. Turn a $\frac{1}{4}$in hem down the outer edge, and pin and tack into place over the original running stitch:

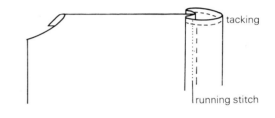

tacking

running stitch

Top stitch with a neat *backstitch* when complete:

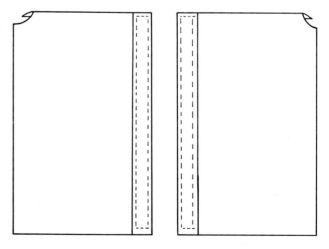

Pin tucking

The front of the cami is decorated with pin tucks, which are very attractive, yet easy to make. Work $\frac{1}{2}$in from the button facings, and fold and pin approximately half a dozen tiny tucks. It is best to tack them with a coloured thread to avoid confusion.

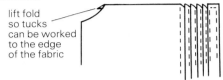

To ensure straight lines, try to work along the vertical threads of the linen. Don't forget – on the paper pattern you allowed only 2 in for pin tucks. Work out how much fabric your tucks take up, or the cami will be too tight.

Fitting
This is a good time to pin the back and two front pieces of the cami together, before beginning the embroidery. Try it on, pinning the front facings together as if buttoned up. Make sure the cami fits comfortably – this is really your last chance to make any small adjustments.

If it is too tight, remove one or two pin tucks. If it feels too loose, even for the blouson effect, you can either trim the underarm seam a little, or add a couple of extra pin tucks.

When you think it is just right, work the pin tucks in a small, firm *running stitch* and remove the coloured tacking.

Front embroidery
The first step is to mark out each front panel for two lines of drawn threadwork. Draw the first about ¾ in after the last pin tuck, and the second approximately the same distance again parallel to it – lines A and B in the diagram.

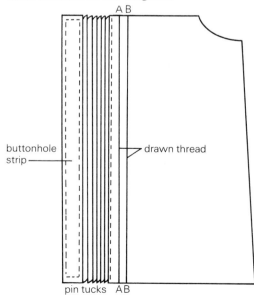

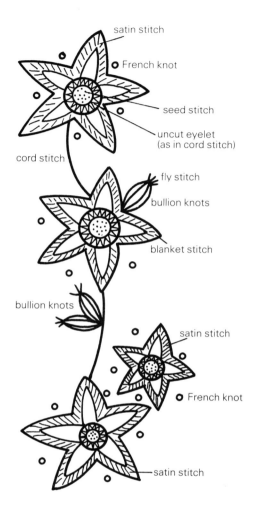

Cami – front embroidery.

Now, using line B as a guide, you can transfer the freestyle embroidery design onto each front panel with carbon paper. It should be slightly off-centre, a little more towards the drawn thread-work than the armhole seam. Remember, too, that the design should be at least 6 in from the bottom of the cami to leave room for the elastic gathering. The design can be worked through using the stitch glossary (pages 107–14).

Drawn threadwork
About five or six threads are drawn for each row of threadwork. If your fabric is fine you may wish to draw out a few more to make a wider panel. As

the threads will be pulled out completely, it is not necessary to darn the edges.

It is easier if you turn the piece sideways and work from right to left on the stitchwork. But do take care to keep an even tension, so that you don't 'shrink' the fabric as you go.

Row A is worked in *zigzag hemstitch*, and row B in *ladder hemstitch* bunched into stars with a central thread of strong machine cotton.

To do this, secure a new long thread on one side of the hem and bind together the first three bars of the ladder, taking care not to pull the work out of shape. Then continue to join bars in groups of three to the end of the row. Don't worry about trying to make the final bars look tidy, as they will eventually be covered by the hemming.

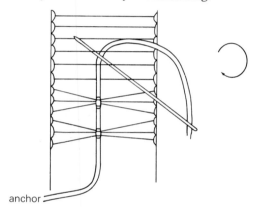

anchor

Seams

French seams are really quite easy, and ideal for fine fabrics. Simply take one of the front panels and pin its underarm edge to the corresponding raw edge of the back of the cami, right sides outwards. I find I fumble less if I do the fixing on a table-top.

Now, allowing a seam of about $\frac{1}{8}$ in, join the two pieces with *running stitch* or *backstitch*, and trim any frayed ends. Press the seam open with a warm iron and fold over, so that the right sides now face each other.

A second seam is pinned so that it completely covers the raw edges of the first – probably about $\frac{1}{4}$ in wide – and tacked. This time backstitch or machine for strength.

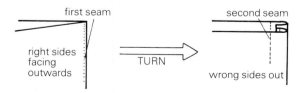

Another method, flat seaming, is to start with the right sides facing each other, but make the seam allowance for the back fractionally narrower than that of the front. Pin and tack, then backstitch or machine $\frac{1}{2}$ in from the front raw edge:

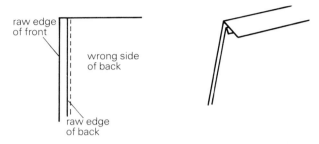

Now fold the wider side of the seam over the narrower:

Then fold again, to give you a tiny double turn in the fabric, pinning as you go.

Finally, flatten the seam down firmly and tack and hem it on the wrong side of the back:

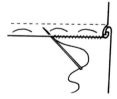

Assembling the facings

We are now almost on the last lap, but there are one or two fiddly bits ahead, so vigilance is required.

The first job is to slip the cami on and pin the shoestring shoulder straps into position, making sure that the whole garment has the loose, but comfortable feel we are aiming for.

When you are happy with it, join the three facing pieces by making two $\frac{1}{2}$ in side seams, machined or *backstitched* for firmness. Open out the seams and press.

Now you can lay out the camisole on a flat surface, and place the completed facing on top of it, right sides together:

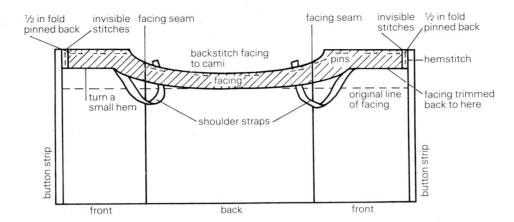

Pin along the top, allowing for just a $\frac{1}{4}$ in seam. At each end, where the facing overlaps the button strips, fold back about a $\frac{1}{2}$ in of the facing and pin.

Around this area, at the extremes of the facing, pinning may prove a little tricky, but don't worry if you have to leave a tiny gap at each end – a few invisible stitches can be worked in later.

Now tack and sew the top of the facing to the cami. I backstitched by hand, because it is easier to manoeuvre and control the fabric.

Where the strap ends peep up through the seam, make an extra row of stitches to hold them firm (and avoid future embarrassment!). Trim the ends if they are too long.

You can now press open the seam and turn the facing completely over to the inside of the camisole. You will see that the facing is a little too long down each side of the button strips. Trim it back to about $2\frac{1}{2}$ in, following the curve of the cami top.

When you are satisfied with the shape of the facing, pin down the folded sides next to the button strips. Follow by turning a small hem on the lower edge of the facing and pin to the camisole.

Now is the time to add those invisible stitches to the outer corners of the facing.

Incidentally, if your facing refuses to lie completely flat when you trim and curve it, don't worry. Simply unpin the hem, flatten it out, and make a few tiny V-shaped snips:

The sides and lower edge of the facing are hemstitched to the camisole.

Hemming the bottom of the cami is, by comparison, very straightforward and quite a relief from all the fumbling and fiddling of the past hour. But make sure it is straight when you pin; if possible, get a second opinion. When you think it hangs nicely, tack down and *hemstitch* along, making a neat finish on the front corners:

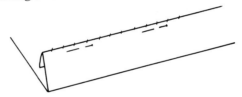

Gathering

Try the cami on and, hands on hips, bunch it where you feel the elastic should go. Mark the spot with a pin and note how far it is from the bottom hem. Using this for reference, make a line of pins round the cami where the elastic is to go.

To make absolutely sure, thread a long piece of cotton and follow the pins with a *running stitch*, leaving the ends hanging loose. You can now slip the cami on again, gently draw in the thread and get an idea of what it will look like.

Now lay an ample length of cotton tape inside the cami, making sure that the centre of it falls along the running stitch. Pin and tack the tape and remove the running thread.

Turn the cami to the right side, and *backstitch* along each side of the tape. I prefer hand sewing everything, but with the end so near in sight, you could machine it. However, don't forget to leave the tape-ends open.

The knicker elastic can now be threaded onto a safety pin and worked through the tape. Secure each end, snip to the right length and cover by stitching down the ends of the tape over it.

Hook and eye

Attach a hook just at the edge of the tape *inside* the front on the buttonhole side. The eye goes on the button side at the edge of the facing. When fastened they should both be invisible. To maintain the cami's authenticity, I covered the eye with a tiny *blanket stitch*.

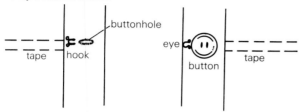

Buttons and buttonholes

If every good story has a beginning, a middle and an end, then every good piece of buttoning should have a top, a middle and a bottom.

The number of buttons on the cami is a question of choice, but there must be one at the top, one in line with the hook and eye, and one somewhere below. Once these are right, the rest can be spaced in proportion.

Begin by laying the righthand-side front facing flat, and place a button at the top. Make a small pencil mark on either side of the button and join with a line:

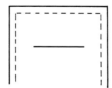

Cut carefully along the line using sharp, pointed scissors. The incision, for a good fit, must not be more than $\frac{1}{8}$ in wider than the button.

Buttonhole stitching

Buttonholes are an important part of the embroidery. Begin by putting two tiny backward stitches on the wrong side, and slip the needle through the slit in the fabric to the topside.

Work your buttonhole stitch from left to right, strengthening the ends with a bar.

When all the buttonholes are finished, use them as a guide for positioning your buttons.

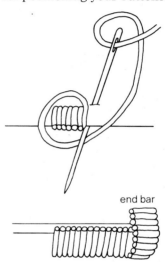

end bar

The camisole is now complete – the product of hours of work, immensely rewarding and beautiful to wear. I have just one final hint: now you've got it, flaunt it.

Stitch Glossary

Backstitch
Make a small backward stitch through the fabric and a longer one on the underside. Work another backward stitch inserting the needle to connect with the last stitch. Follow the design outline, taking care to keep the top stitches evenly sized.

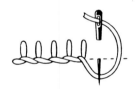

Blanket/buttonhole stitch
Blanket stitch can be used over a folded hem for binding, or as an embroidery stitch. Working from left to right, bring your needle and thread through on the line where the loops are to lie. Insert the needle to make a straight vertical stitch towards the loops. Cover the original thread with the needle which emerges on the line. Draw thread through to form the loop. Repeat, choosing the distance between the stitches to suit your design.

Buttonhole stitch is worked in the same way as blanket stitch, but the stitches are set closer together.

Closed buttonhole stitch
Two stitches form the pattern. This time instead of making vertical stitches towards the loops, sew the first and second stitches slanting towards each other, to form a triangle. Repeat for the third and fourth stitches, and so on.

Buttonhole stitch bars
Essential in cut work to support and retain the design shape.

Two or three long stitches are closely laid along the space to be cut. Secure them to the fabric on either side, maintaining a very firm tension. Taking care not to let your needle catch the fabric, bind the long stitches together with close buttonhole stitches.

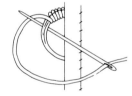

Buttonhole loops
Long stitches, usually made at the edge, take the form of loops. Check they close over the button before covering them with buttonhole stitch.

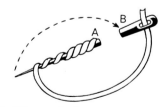

Bullion stitch
Bring the thread through at A and insert needle at B. Allow the point to emerge at A again but do not pull it completely through. Twist the thread around the needle until it resembles a cord long enough to cover the space between A

and B. Hold the twists with your left thumb and carefully draw the needle and thread through. When almost all the thread has been withdrawn, pull the coil gently until it lies flat in the correct position between A and B. Take the thread to the reverse, inserting at B and either make a second stitch or fasten off.

Chain stitch
Needle and thread emerge at point A. Lay the thread in a small loop and hold it with your left thumb. Re-insert the needle at A and bring it out again a little ahead, at B. Be sure the needle comes up through the loop as you draw the thread through. Continue the chain, inserting the needle exactly where the thread last emerged.

Detached chain or lazy daisy stitch
Work as for chain stitch, but instead of continuing the chain, make a small stitch over the

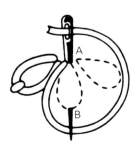

loop to fasten it down. With the thread now at the back of the fabric, either begin another stitch or fasten off.

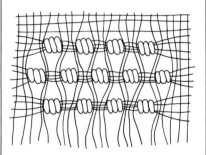

Coil filling stitch
This is a counted thread stitch worked across from right to left. Bind four horizontal threads with three small vertical satin stitches. Pass the needle behind four vertical threads, and then repeat the binding on the next four, pulling the stitches firmly. Continue across the area to be filled and darn in at the back. The second row is again worked right to left, but the coils are worked in alternate spaces.

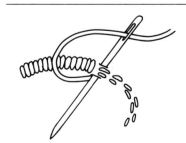

Cord/overcast stitch
Cord stitch The design line is first followed with one or two

lines of running stitch. Then a small, closely-set satin stitch is worked over them, giving the appearance of a narrow cord.

Overcast stitch This is also worked over laid thread. Two or more separate threads emerge at the same point; one is for stitching, and the others are to be laid along the design line and held in place with the left thumb. Closely satin stitch over the laid threads. At the end of the design take *all* the threads to the reverse to fasten off.

Couching
Lay one thread along the outline, as in overcast stitch, and hold in place with your left thumb. But instead of completely covering it, make small single binding stitches at evenly spaced intervals.

Bokhara couching
This is an attractive filling stitch. Work with one thread and make a long stitch across the design area. Then bring the needle to the surface and make a small stitch to tie it down. Work a longer stitch on the reverse and continue tying down with evenly spaced stitches. Where

it is not practical to continue couching, for instance, at small corners and points, finish with satin stitching.

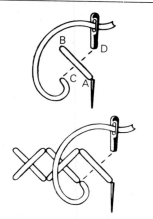

Cross stitch

There are many ways of doing cross stitch, depending upon the effect you want. When worked on canvas it is sometimes, rather grandly, called Gros Point. Make a small slanted stitch from A to B. On the reverse, point the needle in a vertical line to emerge at C. Cross over the first slant and insert the needle at D.

To make a row of cross stitches, work single slanted stitches. Complete by returning to cross each original slant.

Double cross stitch

Work a single cross stitch. Then cover it with a vertical stitch followed by a horizontal one.

Sometimes a small binding stitch is made, to hold the

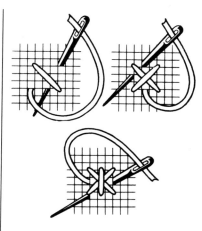

centre. This can be a horizontal stitch, or a tiny cross. When worked in this way it is sometimes called star stitch.

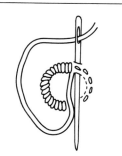

Eyelets

This is a tiny circle outline, worked in cord stitch.

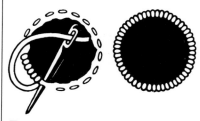

Eyelet holes

Work a row of small running stitch round the circle. Pierce the centre with a stiletto and fold back the ragged edge. Closely overcast the folded edge and running stitch. Trim away any ragged edge at the back.

Larger circles or longer eyelet holes may be cut across the centre both ways and the cut

ends folded back, instead of piercing with a stiletto.

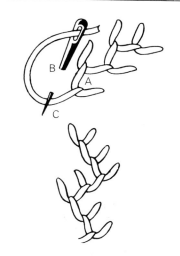

Feather stitch

The thread emerges at A and, working right to left, the needle is inserted at B. Pull the thread through gently to make a small loop. Now bring the needle through at C, and repeat. Work a few loops to the left before changing direction.

To work to the right, starting with your thread in the centre of the previous loop, insert your needle to form a curve to the right, to form a zigzag pattern.

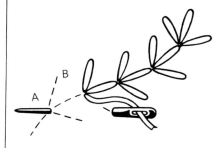

Fern stitch

Three evenly-sized straight stitches all emerge from point A and fan out. Work A to B, then return to A, and so on.

This stitch can be worked right to left to form a row.

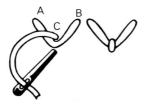

Fly stitch

The thread comes through at A and the needle is inserted at B. Pull the thread through gently, then bring the needle through at C to tie down the loop, forming a 'V' shape.

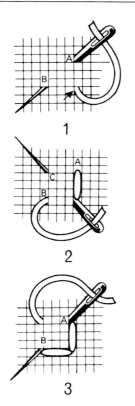

1

2

3

Four-sided stitch

This stitch is worked from right to left and can be used as a border or a filling. Bring the thread through at the arrow; insert the needle at A (four threads up), bring it through at B (four threads down and four to the left). Insert at the arrow, bring out at C (four threads up and four threads to

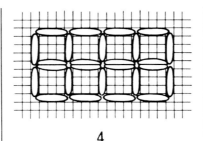

4

the left of A). Insert again at A and bring out at B. Continue in this way to the end of the row or close the end for a single four-sided stitch. For filling stitch. Turn the fabric round for next and all following rows and work in the same way. Pull all stitches firmly.

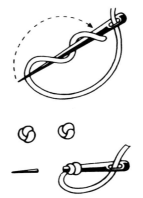

French knots

Bring the thread to the surface at the point at which you wish to place the knot. Hold the thread with your left hand and wind the needle once or twice around the thread close to the fabric. Twist the needle-point and insert it back into the fabric where it first emerged. Keep a firm hold on the thread with the left thumb, for as long as possible while you draw the thread through at the back. Secure on the wrong side for a single knot, or continue.

Gros Point stitch

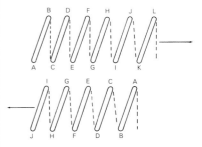

Usually worked on canvas as a full – or perhaps more commonly as a half–cross stitch.

Bring the thread through at A and make a slanting stitch upwards to B, with a vertical stitch on the reverse to C. Continue working across in rows.

(Trammed Gros Point stitch is more suitable for canvas with a very open weave. It is the same as Gros Point stitch, but is worked over a horizontally laid thread. Work on a frame to keep a firm tension.)

The second row is worked right to left, and looks identical to the first row. This time working from A, slant downwards to B, with a vertical stitch on the reverse, pointing upwards to C.

Hemstitch (as in plain sewing)

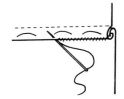

Insert your needle through the folded hem. Catch a tiny stitch in the single fabric, and in the same movement insert the needle into the fold, before drawing the thread through. Keep the spacing and size of your stitches even and continue along the hemline.

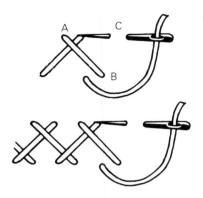

Herringbone stitch

This embroidery stitch is sometimes used for hemming, as it will bind a raw edge and hem down at the same time. Work left to right, making a small slanting stitch from A down to B, where the needle catches the fabric, before making an upward slanting stitch to C. Then it again catches the fabric before moving on to the next stitch. Continue in this manner.

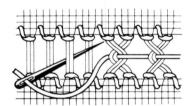

Fig. 1

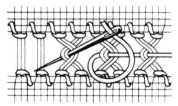

Fig. 2

Interlaced hemstitch

Work ladder hemstitch first. Fasten a long thread at the right-hand side centred on the loose threads.
Fig. 1 – Pass the working thread across the front of two groups of threads and insert the needle from left to right under the second group.
Fig. 2 – Twist the second group over the first group by inserting the needle under the first group from right to left. Pull thread through. The interlaced thread should be pulled firmly to lie in position through the centre of the twisted groups.

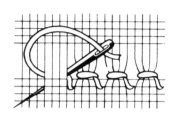

Hemstitch

Measure required depth of hem, plus the turnings and withdraw required number of threads. Do not withdraw the threads right across fabric, but only to form a square or rectangle. Cut threads at the centre and withdraw gradually outwards on each side to within the hem measurement, leaving a sufficient length of thread at corners in order to darn the ends invisibly. Turn back the hem to the space of the drawn threads, mitre corners and baste. Bring the working thread out two fabric threads down from the drawn threads, and through the folded hem, at the right-hand side. Pass the needle behind four loose threads, then insert the needle behind the same four threads, bringing the needle out two threads down through all the folds of the hem in readiness for the next stitch. The number of threads may be varied to suit the fabric or design.

Ladder hemstitch

This stitch is worked in the same way as hemstitch, with the hemstitch being worked along

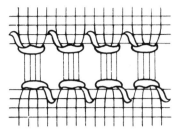

both edges of the space of drawn threads.
Hemstitch and ladder hemstitch may be worked on fine linen or even-weave linen.

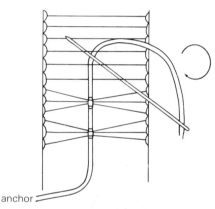

anchor

Ladder hemstitch – bound

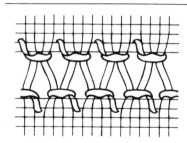

Zigzag hemstitch

This variation is worked in the same way as hemstitch, but there must be an even number of threads in each group of loose threads caught together in the first row. In the second row, the groups are divided in half, so that each group is composed of half the number of threads from one group and half from the adjacent group. A half group starts and ends the second row.

Long and short stitch
Worked as satin stitch, except that the stitches are unevenly sized. It is especially useful for filling large and/or irregularly-shaped designs, and for obtaining a shaded effect.

Work the outline first, using evenly-sized satin stitches where possible. At the edge of the shape, you will probably have to alter the stitch size accordingly.

Where the design is in sections, for example, a flower head, work each section separately, to maintain perspective and shade.

This is a good stitch for using graded shades of colour, as the colour change is gradual and more natural.

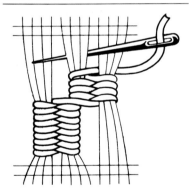

Needleweaving
Withdraw the number of threads required for the pattern. When using a thick embroidery thread and a fairly heavy fabric, one row of weaving (back and forward) is usually sufficient to replace one drawn thread of fabric. Work blocks of weaving to fill the space, with an even

number of stitches in each block. The blocks are worked diagonally across the loose threads. The diagram shows how the connecting stitch is worked over and under to start the new block.

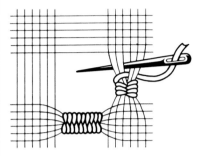

Woven bars
This bar can also be used in drawn thread embroidery. To work woven bars, withdraw an even number of threads from the fabric and separate the loose threads into bars by weaving over and under an even number of threads until the threads are completely covered.

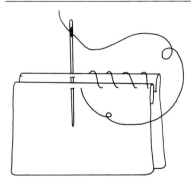

Oversewing (as in plain sewing)
This is a plain sewing stitch used to join two folded edges. I usually work from left to right and for a really strong finish stitch again right to left.

The needle is passed through both folds in one movement catching only the edge of the fabric. Continue in this way, drawing the thread through firmly to hold the folds together.

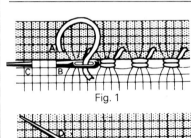

Petit Point stitch
This, sometimes called tent stitch, is beautifully simple and used on many of the old embroideries. The stitch can be worked vertically, diagonally or horizontally. It is best to work across the design for small isolated patches.

Use on single thread canvas, and work the first row right to left. The stitch slants upwards to the right on the surface, and a longer slanting stitch is taken on the reverse to C, and so on.

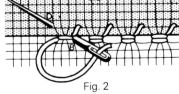

The second row is worked left to right and on the surface looks identical to the first row. This time beginning at the top of the stitch slant downwards to the left for the surface and take a longer slanting stitch upwards to the right on the reverse.

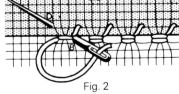

Fig. 1

Fig. 2

Pin stitch
This stitch is mainly a drawn fabric stitch, but it can be used in drawn thread embroidery and

for outlining appliqué work. Fig. 1 – For a hem edge, bring the thread through the folded hem at A, insert the needle at B and bring out at C; insert once more at B and bring out at C. Fig. 2 – Insert again at B, bring out through the folded hem at D. Continue in this way to end of row. Pull all stitches firmly.

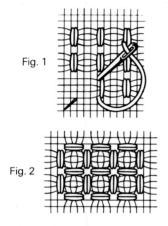

Fig. 1

Fig. 2

Punch stitch

Fig. 1 – Work two straight stitches into the same place over four threads, then bring the needle out four threads down and four threads to the left in readiness for the next stitch. Work along the row in this way. Turn the fabric for next and each successive row.
Fig. 2 – The squares are completed by turning the fabric sideways and working in the same way.

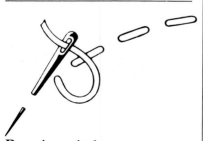

Running stitch

This is probably the simplest stitch of all the straight stitches.

The thread is taken through to the right side and stitching follows the design line. Make a small straight stitch on the surface, and a smaller stitch catching up the underside. Keep both top and underneath stitches regular for a pleasing finish.

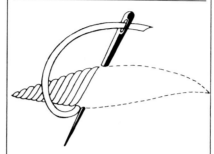

Satin stitch

Basically simple, this stitch is worked in many different ways to create various effects. Straight stitches are closely worked to cover a design shape. Take care to form a neat edge as you sew.

It may be worked vertically, or slanted across the design.

Where the design is drawn in sections, fill one section at a time.

By slanting the stitching for each section at different angles, you can create a more realistic finish.

Padded satin stitch

A groundwork of random running stitches is laid, which produces a raised effect when covered with satin stitch. Take

running stitch

the thread to the starting point and satin stitch over the running stitch.

(Detached chain stitch may also be used for the padding.)

For a beautifully rounded edge to your satin stitching, outline the design shape in split stitch before covering with satin stitch.

Seeding stitch

A simple filling stitch which can be used where a less solid effect is desired. It creates a haze of tiny stitches. Keep the top stitches evenly sized and place them at random within the design shape.

Alternatively, they can be used to fill the background – throwing the shape into relief.

Sheaf stitch

Another attractive filling stitch. Make three vertical satin stitches and bind them together in the centre before inserting the needle and passing onto the next sheaf. Work in either direction across the design, setting the sheaves in alternate positions for each row.

Split stitch

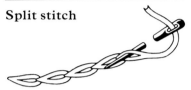

Working left to right make a small straight stitch along the design line. Then take a smaller backward stitch on the reverse, which splits the top stitch as it emerges. Draw the thread through and repeat. Keep the stitching regular to produce a fine, flat finish.

Star filling stitch
See *Double cross stitch* fastened down by a central cross.

Stem stitch

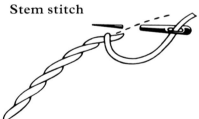

Work from left to right, taking regular, slightly slanting stitches along the line of the design. The thread always emerges on the left side of the previous stitch. This stitch is used for flower stems, outlines, etc. It can also be used as a filling: rows of stem stitch are worked closely together within a shape until it is filled completely.

Straight stitch
Sometimes called single satin stitch, this stitch is used only to cover small straight lines.
The stitches are placed singly

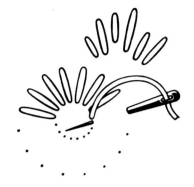

and may vary in length and direction.

Tacking stitch

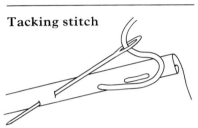

For the temporary stitch used in plain sewing, a special soft thread is available.
Do tack with care as the finished effect is so much better. Use evenly spaced stitches that are larger on top than underneath. When tacking curves or tricky pieces, use smaller stitches.
This stitch is sometimes used as a filling stitch. Work the stitches in alternate rows, set closely together.

Twisted insertion stitch

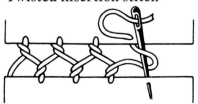

A small stitch is taken alternately on each piece of

fabric to be joined. The needle always enters the fabric from beneath and is twisted once round the thread before making the next stitch, on the opposite piece of fabric.

Woven bars
See *Needleweaving*.

Zigzag hemstitch
See *Ladder hemstitch*.

Metric Conversion

Like many other needlewomen, I was brought up to think in inches and yards, and you will notice that I refer to imperial measurements.

Converting from one to the other is quite simple (especially if you have a tape measure with inches on one side and centimetres on the other!).

Here is an approximate and general conversion guide which may help when shopping.

Fabric widths

inches to centimetres:

36 in	or	90cm
44/45 in	or	114cm
48 in	or	122cm
54 in	or	137cm
60 in	or	152cm

Fabric lengths

inches to centimetres:

9 in or $\frac{1}{4}$ yd = 23cm

18 in or $\frac{1}{2}$ yd = 46cm

27 in or $\frac{3}{4}$ yd = 69cm

36 in or 1 yd = 91$\frac{1}{2}$cm

12 in or $\frac{1}{3}$ yd = 28cm

24 in or $\frac{2}{3}$ yd = 61cm

centimetres to inches:

25cm or $\frac{1}{4}$ metre = 10 in

50cm or $\frac{1}{2}$ metre = 19$\frac{3}{4}$ in

75cm or $\frac{3}{4}$ metre = 29$\frac{1}{2}$ in

100cm or 1 metre = 39$\frac{1}{4}$ in

33$\frac{1}{3}$cm or $\frac{1}{3}$ metre = 13 in

66$\frac{2}{3}$cm or $\frac{2}{3}$ metre = 26$\frac{1}{4}$ in

Stockists

Your local needlework shop or department store haberdashery counter are the best sources of materials – and usually full of surprises.

If, however, you really do have difficulty tracking something down, there are some stockists who run a mail order service. Others I mention simply because they are worth a visit if you ever get the chance to go there.

General

Royal School of Needlework,
25 Princes Gate,
London SW7 1QE

The shop here is open to the public, and an absolute haven for the needlewoman. I love it so much I could take a Thermos and sandwiches and stay there all day. Beth Russell, who runs the shop, is a source of inspiration and help. I can't think of any equipment they don't stock – and there is an excellent mail order service.

Open Mon.–Fri., 9.30–5.30.

The Danish House,
16 Sloane Street,
London SW1

This houses an enormous collection of tools and more than 1000 embroidery designs under one roof. It is better, perhaps, for browsing as their catalogue caters heavily for counted stitch needlework.

Magnifying glasses

The Easy-View magnifying glass hangs round the neck and rests on the chest, and is a wonderful help for close work, which is tiring on the eyes. Available from the Royal School of Needlework shop, or direct from

Combined Optical Industries Ltd,
198 Bath Road,
Slough,
Bucks.

Fabrics

Limericks (Linens) Ltd,
Limerick House,
117 Victoria Avenue,
Southend-on-Sea,
Essex SS2 6EL

Limericks are a real find for fabric-hunters. They operate a fast, efficient mail-order-only service – and the catalogue is free. They are specialists in linens of all kinds (they do a nice cream Irish embroidery linen in 36 in and 54 in widths). They offer everything from sheeting to make your own bed linen, to fine natural fabrics for embroidery. Hard-to-find fabrics are usually in stock.

Liberty's,
Regent Street,
London W1

A haven of tranquil inspiration. The sheer joy of wandering around acres of fine silks and fabrics sets the mind working overtime. Like Mecca, at least one pilgrimage is essential in every needlewoman's life.

Open Mon.–Fri., 9–5.30; Thurs., 9–7; Sat., 9–5.

Central London Stores,
100–106 Mackenzie Road,
London N7

Linen and natural fabric off-cuts, job lots and oddments: the Myers' rambling family warehouse is full of them and, although they don't really run a mail order service as such, they are extremely friendly and will post individual orders anywhere. Prices are cheap. If they don't have what you want, ring the following week and it is invariably in.

Beads

Creative Beadcraft Ltd,
Unit 26,
Chiltern Trading Estate,
Earl Howe Road,
Holmer Green,
High Wycombe,
Bucks HP15 6QT

They possibly have the most mind-boggling array of mail-order beads anywhere. The catalogue costs £2, but when you see it you realize why – it bulges with samples, all sewn into the pages by hand.

The selection is a postal version of stock carried by:

Ells and Farrier,
5 Princes Street,
Hanover Square,
London W1

Callers-only at this tiny glittering cave crammed with every kind of bead imaginable.

Herb pillow

For ideas on how to fill your herb pillow, try a booklet from:

The Herb Society,
34 Boscobel Place,
London SW1

Culpepper's, the herb people, have a mail order department at:

Hadstock Road,
Linton,
Cambridgeshire CB1 6NJ

They sell ready-mixed sleep herbs and pot pourris, and everything you need to mix your own.

Stitch books

I must have read every one available, but the best are still published by J. & P. Coats. My bible is their *50 Freestyle Embroidery Stitches* and *50 Counted Thread Embroidery Stitches*, which fit neatly into my handbag.

Another classic is their *100 Embroidery Stitches*, also bag-size; it is perhaps the most comprehensive single volume on the market.

Kits

If you are trying your hand at needlework for the first time, you may wish to purchase a kit before taking the plunge and designing your own pictures.

I find Penelope the best and most comprehensive around. Their tapestry range starts at very simple Premier kits for children and beginners, right through to the Gold Collection, which are beautifully packed and make a lovely gift.

If you have a taste for tapestry they are ideal, containing everything you need – from canvas and silks, right down to a needle!

The Gold Collection is made up mostly of classic tapestry designs. Penelope's Main Range, packed in tubes, has around 100 patterns to choose from, all of approximately the same degree of difficulty.

A general guideline for tapestry, if you are buying for the first time, is that bigger designs are usually more complex than smaller ones, with frequent colour changes. Smaller kits – such as Penelope's Premier range – tend to be simpler and more confidence-inspiring for the absolute beginner.

They also produce an excellent range of embroidery kits – I particularly like their Edwardian range, with ten nostalgic designs taken from old photographs and postcards.

If you catch the bug and would like to build a collection as you gain experience, it is often better to buy something from a series, such as their Chinese styles, or a very collectable series of flowers, butterflies and birds.

Penelope kits, almost without exception, are on natural fabrics, such as cotton or linen and – like your own needlework designs – will last for years.

Acknowledgments

We would like to thank: J. & P. Coats (UK) Ltd for permission to use drawings from their stitch books, in the book and in the Stitch Glossary; the Royal School of Needlework for their help and advice during the preparation of the manuscript; and Helen Conrad for her help.

Photographs by Tom Mannion; decorative paintwork by Joyce Manley.

Line drawings by Kevin Maddison.